ART AND HISTORY OF
TUSCANY

A land rich in flavours and colours.
A region where the history and culture have produced a delicious
tradition of food and wine.

BONECHI

D1501846

Publication created and designed by Casa Editrice Bonechi. *Editorial management:* Serena de Leonardis. *Graphic design and layout:* Serena de Leonardis. *Make up:* M&M, Firenze, Teresa Donato. *Picture research:* Serena de Leonardis. *Cover:* Manuela Ranfagni. *Texts by the Casa Editrice Bonechi Editorial Department. Translations and revised texts by* Eve Leckey. *Editing:* Anna Baldini *Drawings:* Francesco Bombardi *(p. 26 below, 90 centre)*; Paolo Fiumi *(p. 38 above, 62 above)*. *Cover: cartography by* Sauro Giampaia.

© Copyright by Casa Editrice Bonechi, via Cairoli 18/b, Firenze - Italia. E-mail: bonechi@bonechi.it

The majority of the photographs are property of the Casa Editrice Bonechi Archives.
They were taken by AA.VV./Doriano Ciapetti/Luca del Pia/Italfotogieffe (Archivio Fotografico Toscana Qui); Gaetano Barone, Carlo Cantini, Comitato per le ricerche sulla cultura materiale della Toscana, Serena De Leonardis, Andrea Fantauzzo, Alessandro Ferrini, Foto Grassi, Foto Sovrintendenza Archeologica per la Toscana, Fotowiemer, Franco Frilli, Sergio Galeotti, Roberto Germogli, Paolo Giambone, Gianluca Guetta, Silvano Guerrini, Italfotogieffe, Cesare Moroni, MSA, Niccolò Orsi Battaglini, Andrea Pistolesi, Antonio Quattrone, Renata Sistemi (p. 6 below, a courtesy of), Renato Stopani, Aldo Umicini.
Other photographs were provided by
Andrea Innocenti: *p. 97 centre, 98 above, 127 below*; Atlantide (Guido Cozzi): *p. 5, 123 above left*; Patrizia Del Duca: *p. 63*; Foto Scala: *p. 29 below, 46 above, 49, 69, 73 above left, 113 above right, 120 below left*; Francesco Giannoni: *p. 36/37, 96 below, 97 below left*; Sergio Galeotti: *p. 44 below, 46 below, 47 above, 48 below, 50 centre and below*; Istituzione Giostra del Saracino e Servizio Giostra del Saracino e folclore, Comune di Arezzo/ Piero Vannuccini *(a courtesy of): p. 73 centre and below*; Fabio Turbanti *(a courtesy of): p. 51*.

The publisher apologises for any omissions and is willing to make amends with the formal recognition of the author of any photo subsequently identified.

ISBN 88-476-1792-8

www. bonechi.com

TUSCANY
historic outline

There is no doubt that in prehistoric times many areas of Tuscany were already inhabited, as witnessed by interesting items discovered in the territories of Arezzo, of Siena (Palaeolithic) and in the rest of the region (Neolithic and metal age). The historic period began around 1500 B.C., during the lengthy period of the bronze age, and finds include pottery, tools and weapons in stone, bone and metal. The Villanovan culture belongs to the Iron Age (9th-8th cent. B.C.) and is the prelude to the birth here of the great Etruscan civilization. In the 7th and 6th centuries B.C. the Etruscans extended their dominion beyond the current borders of the region and occupied parts of Lazio, Campania, Umbria, the valley of the Po and Corsica. During these centuries the Etruscans therefore controlled a large portion of the peninsula and brought a high degree of civilization and progress to the areas they ruled. But in the 5th-4th centuries B.C. they were attacked by other peoples who, in the meantime, had grown in power and culture. They gave way to the Greek and Carthaginian supremacy of the seas, and to the Celts and Romans on land and were eventually forced to stipulate peace treaties with the Romans, who were the new political power in the peninsula. The policy adopted by the Romans in Etruria was particularly intelligent and permitted the conquered Etruscan cities to retain partial autonomy. They also financed numerous public works (among others, they linked Etruria to the most important communication routes). Even so the region slowly and inexorably declined as the population continued to diminish. At the beginning of the Imperial age, Tuscany became the seventh region of the Roman Empire. In the 3rd century A.D., under the reign of Diocletian, Etruria, now known as Tuscia, was joined to Umbria. In the early Middle Ages Tuscia's decline, which was to continue under Lombard rule, set in. Once-flourishing centres such as Lucca, Pisa, Arezzo and Florence became ever less important. The arrival of the Franks (A.D. 774) marked a turn for the better. The region was divided into feuds and with feudalism the abandoned cities of Tuscia slowly came back to life. The Crusades meant new life for one city in particular - Pisa. A city on the sea, and therefore favoured in trade, Pisa was the centre where the various Tuscan feudatories met before setting sail for the East from the city's port. In the meantime other Tuscan cities, in particular Florence (in the field of textiles), and Siena (for banking activities), began to acquire power. With the passage from the feudal period to that of the communes, Tuscia, by now called Toscana, began a long period marked by struggles between rival cities: these were the years of the Guelphs and the Ghibellines, of antagonism between Florence and Pisa, between Siena and Florence. The city which gradually succeeded in coming to the fore was Florence and by the early 14th century it was the most powerful in the region. Even proud Pisa was forced to surrender to this most powerful of Tuscan cities in 1406. With free access to the sea, Florence was now politically and economically independent. The only cities which still resisted were the small but robust republics of Siena and Lucca. During the 15th century, the Medici, rich and intelligent Florentine bankers, took power and transformed the communal status of Florence into a principality, and in the second half of the 16th century, under Cosimo I de' Medici, it officially became the Grand Duchy of Tuscany, now including Siena and Lucca, which had also been forced to surrender. This was the beginning of a long period of great success for the region. The opulence of Florence, which was also reflected in the other Tuscan cities, permitted the region to live the greatest period in its history. During the periods of Humanism and the Renaissance, Florence and Tuscany became the cradle of international culture. In 1737 the last of the Medici Grand Dukes, Gian Gastone, ceded the sceptre of the Grand Duchy to the Lorraine dynasty, who continued to govern with intelligence and liberalism. As a result of great changes in the international scene at the end of the 18th century and of Napoleon's rise to power, the Grand Duchy of Tuscany was annexed to the French Empire until Bonaparte's fall. Then came the Risorgimento and the revolutionary movements for the Union of Italy, and in 1860 Tuscany was annexed to the new Kingdom of Italy. Five years later Florence became the capital of the new nation and remained such until 1871. At the beginning of the 20th century the population began to increase and the towns of Tuscany started to develop; these were the years tormented by the "social question", the vindications of the rights of workers and the birth of fascism. In World War II, Tuscany took an active part in the struggle for liberation and, with the end of the war, began an energetic campaign of reconstruction, facilitating speedy industrialization.

Tuscan Traditions

The fertile hills of Tuscany and the historic towns with their wealth of centuries-old art still evoke the feeling of an easy, natural lifestyle that seems ever more difficult to achieve. During the 20th century the age-old relationship between man and nature changed profoundly in proportion to technological developments and the urbanization of the rural population; values and knowledge specific to that particular social group have become no more than a memory, conserved like historical artefacts by the population.

Today, our approach to the countryside and aspects of rural life is a cultural one and we view it in the same way that we would consider a monument or work of art, as if in this way we can preserve the pleasure that this fascinating "masterpiece" is capable of evoking, particularly when the past is as well preserved as here in the Tuscan countryside.

Rediscovery of the countryside has given rise to a series of initiatives aimed at promoting the region's local produce. Cultural itineraries and wine and gastronomic tours now exist, while many farm museums have come into being, such as those in Villafranca Lunigiana, Antella, San Pellegrino in Alpe, Capannori and the Ethnological Museum in Massa.

A typical Tuscan farmhouse deep in the countryside.

Cypress trees and grapevines alternate harmoniously in the Tuscan countryside.

Tuscan Farmhouse

The typical Tuscan farmhouse that developed throughout the region from the 18th century onwards, was first built in brick during the 16th century and took as its model the stone-built medieval gentleman's country residence. These were often allocated to the farm workers thus representing a genuine improvement to the quality of rural life and an exception compared to other regions. A survival from medieval days, they often had one or two towers, or a tower used as a dovecote. The most classic style is that of a building which is regular and harmonious in form, reflecting the architectural canons of the Renaissance. Reorganization of the rural landscape lead to the development of scattered settlements and the farmer's house became the hub of the estate, created to ensure the autonomy of the family, that crucial element of rural socio-economic organization where a strict division of work and sharing goods and produce applied.

The house was conceived as a structure divided into separate areas for the various kinds of work and for more domestic functions. There was a barn outside and a well or tank for fresh water, as well as a vegetable

A veritable mountain of flasks of wine arriving in Piazza Poggi in Florence.

Oxen yoked to a cart carrying fodder

There is no doubt that in Tuscany the peasant culture achieved an extremely high degree of organization. In this and the following pages are some photos from the last century showing aspects of agricultural work and production: below, an old threshing machine at work.

garden with its own source of water, a washing trough, pigsty, chicken run and there was almost always a yard in front of the house where threshing took place and the haystack was made. Below ground was a cellar while the stables, drying rooms, stores for tools and carts, and the larders for farm produce were on the ground level, which often had a floor of beaten earth. A canopy or loggia on one or two floors provided space and shelter for domestic tasks such as spinning wool and sewing. The oven was often under a loggia on the ground floor. The kitchen, the heart of the rural house, was in the middle of the first floor and the doors into the bedrooms lead off it. The only source of heat was the hearth and friends and neighbours gathered here to pass the long winter evenings. "Official" family decisions were made around the large table in the evening and everyone participated in the frugal supper, the only real meal of the day.

Countryside around the village of Capalbio in the Maremma.

Dusting off freshly baked bread.

A haystack in the farmyard.

Reaping corn.

If anything was left over, portions for breakfast the next day were made up by the wife of the house who saw to its general organization. The most common and basic element in a farmer's diet was bread, made from wholemeal and rich in minerals, vitamins and protein, while all other forms of food were generically known as "companatico" - an accompaniment to the essential bread.

Once a week 20-25 loaves of 2 kg were baked for about 10 people, an average family. Seasonings were oil and vinegar, sparingly used. The characteristics of typical Tuscan cooking are derived from these ancient culinary foundations – plain and unsophisticated dishes to be enjoyed with a good wine, such as the simple old meals still found today: pappa al pomodoro (tomato bread soup), minestra di pane (vegetable bread soup), acquacotta (onion and garlic soup), food that is as simple and natural as its origins.

FLORENCE

*T*he river Arno cuts its way through the broad plain on which Florence lies, surrounded by the splendid hills of the Tusco-Emilian Apennines. Already occupied in prehistoric times, as early as the 8th century B.C. an Italic people with a Villanovan culture settled in the area between the Arno and Mugnone rivers, but little is known of these remote times. In 59 B.C. the Roman city was founded with the square ground plan of the *castrum*. The *decumanus maximus* was laid out along what are now the Via del Corso, Via degli Speziali and Via Strozzi, while the ancient *cardo* corresponds to the line between Piazza San Giovanni, Via Roma and Via Calimala. With the arrival of the barbarians, Florence was first besieged by the Ostrogoths (405) of Radagaisus, who plundered the surrounding countryside although Florence managed to resist, and Stilicho's troops inflicted an overwhelming defeat on the enemy. Next came the Byzantines, who occupied Florence in 539, and the Goths who took over the city in 541. Under Lombard domination (570) it managed to safeguard its autonomy, while under the Franks the number of inhabitants diminished and the city lost most of its territories. Around the year 1000, the city (whose symbol is a lily) began to develop and this continued for various centuries in spite of numerous controversies, wars and internecine struggles. New walls surrounded the city, new civic and religious buildings went up, and at the same time the arts, literature, and trade continued to prosper. In 1183 the city became a free commune, even though it had already actually availed itself of this freedom for many years. The first clashes between the two factions, Guelph and Ghibelline, date from this period. The former were followers of the Pope, the latter of the Emperor. The ensuing struggles were to lacerate the civil structure of the city up to 1268. Despite the unstable social and political situation, this period witnessed an upsurge in the arts and in literature. This was the time of Dante and the "*dolce stil novo*", of Giotto and Arnolfo di Cambio. In the 15th century the city's rise continued. Florence was a trading city but also the new cradle for Italian, and eventually European, culture.

Many powerful families (the Pitti, Frescobaldi, Strozzi, Albizi) vied for supremacy in the city and one soon took control. The powerful Medici, a family of bankers that began with the founder Cosimo , later known as the Elder, were to govern up to the first half of the 18th century, transforming Florence into a beacon during the period of Humanism and the Renaissance. Great personalities such as Leonardo da Vinci and Michelangelo characterized the period and Florentine prestige reached its zenith. In 1737 the Medicis gave way to the house of Lorraine and the government continued along the lines of moderate liberalism even if at that point the great period of Florentine culture was on the wane. In 1860, during the Risorgimento, Tuscany was annexed to the Kingdom of Italy with a plebiscite. For a brief period Florence then became the capital of the new nation.

PONTE VECCHIO

The oldest bridge in the city, it was built in 1345 by Neri di Fioravante and the elegant three-arched span remains unchanged. A characteristic feature of the bridge is the row of small houses on either side. At the centre of the bridge, the buildings are interrupted and an opening furnishes a fine view of the Arno and the other bridges.

A bronze bust of *Benvenuto Cellini* has been placed here. Above the houses, on the upstream side of the bridge, is **Vasari's Corridor**, built by Vasari so that Cosimo could reach Palazzo Pitti from Palazzo Vecchio.

The elegant arches on Ponte Vecchio.

The arches of the Santa Trinita bridge with Ponte Vecchio in the background.

THE CATHEDRAL

The Cathedral of Santa Maria del Fiore is the creation of the talent and commitment of many artists who worked, on it over several centuries, beginning in 1296 such as Arnolfo di Cambio, Giotto, Andrea Pisano and Brunelleschi. Arnolfo's **façade** was torn down in 1587 and designs for a new one abounded. Yet it was not until 1871 that the plans by De Fabris were approved and they were finally carried out in 1887. Above the three portals with *Stories from the Life of the Virgin* are three lunettes with, left to right, *Charity*, the *Madonna with the Patrons of the City,* and *Faith*. The gable of the main entrance has a *Madonna in Glory*. Statues of the *Apostles* and of the *Virgin* form the frieze between the rose windows at the side and the one in the centre. The tympanum with a bas-relief of *God the Father* is set above a row of busts of artists. In the interior there is a strong feeling for space, both vertical and horizontal, in keeping with the dictates of Italian Gothic architecture. The aisles flow into the area of the high altar around which the three apses or tribunes, each divided into five parts, radiate. Under the stained glass designed by Ghiberti and Paolo Uccello's *Clock* (1443), the **interior façade** bears the 14th-century lunette with the *Coronation of the Virgin* by Gaddo Gaddi, and the *tomb of Antonio d'Orso,* by Tino di Camaino, dated around 1321. The **left aisle** houses various masterpieces of art: at the beginning is the aedicule with a statue of *Joshua*, by Ciuffagni, Donatello and Nanni di Bartolo, and the neighbouring *aedicule of S. Zanobius* painted at the end of the 14th century by Vanni del Biondo. Between Benedetto da Maiano's *bust of A. Squarcialupi* and *equestrian monuments,* are detached frescoes of *Giovanni Acuto* (John Hawkwood) and *Niccolò da Tolentino* by Paolo Uccello and Andrea del Castagno respectively.

In front of the arch of the fourth bay are the panels with SS. *Cosmas and Damian* (by Bicci di Lorenzo, 15th cent.) and *Dante* (by Domenico di Michelino, 1465).

Two marble aedicules flank the door of the **Sacrestia Nuova** (New Sacristy) with a lunette in glazed terracotta by Luca della Robbia of the *Ressurection of Christ*. On the opposite side, beyond the *high altar* - a 16th-century work by Baccio Bandinelli - there is, in mirror image, the door of the **Sacrestia Vecchia** (Old Sacristy) with a lunette of the *Ascension* by Luca della Robbia. The right tribune contains a Giottesque fresco with the *Madonna* and a *St. Philip* by Bandini. Beyond this in the south aisle is a painting of *St. Bartholomew Enthroned* by Franchi (15th cent.) and the aedicule with a *Prophet* by Nanni di Banco (1408), set between a

roundel of Giotto (Benedetto da Maiano, 1490) and a bust of Brunelleschi (Buggiano, 1446). Here a modern staircase descends to the pre-existent church of Santa Reparata.

Santa Reparata was situated where the front part of the cathedral now stands. The church had been built in the 4th-5th centuries on the ruins of a Roman *domus*. At the time of the Byzantine wars the church was destroyed and then rebuilt between the 8th and 9th centuries. Between the year 1000 and 1100 a crypt with a raised choir was created in the area of the apse, which was flanked on the outside by two bell towers.

The great **dome** of the Cathedral of S. Maria del Fiore, which Brunelleschi had intended to be unadorned, was however painted by Giorgio Vasari and Zuccari between 1572 and 1579. Scenes from the *Last Judgement* are set in three concentric bands with the *Prophets* at the top of the vault in a *trompe l'oeil* lantern with a railing.

BAPTISTERY

Built during the 4th - 5th centuries and in 1293 reconstructed as it appears today, the **exterior** of the Baptistery is faced with white and green marble. The three sets of bronze doors are particularly important. The **South Doors**, which are the oldest and are decorated with scenes from the *Life of St. John the Baptist* and the *Allegories of the Theological and Cardinal Virtues*, are by Ándrea Pisano (1130-1336). The **North Doors** with *Stories from the New Testament*, *Evangelists* and *Doctors of the Church* are by Lorenzo Ghiberti (1403-1424), with the help of Donatello,

The Baptistery

A view across Florence with the Cathedral and Giotto's bell tower in the centre, Palazzo Vecchio on the right and Orsanmichele on the left.

Bernardo Ciuffagni, Paolo Uccello and Bernardo Cennini. The **East Doors** known as the *"Gates of Paradise"* with ten panels (now replaced by copies, while the originals are in the **Museo dell'Opera del Duomo**) which represent *Stories from the Old Testament*. The work of Lorenzo Ghiberti, this composition is one of the greatest masterpieces of 15th-century sculpture. The **interior** has an inlaid pavement with decorative motifs of eastern derivation. On the walls from left to right: a Roman *sarcophagus,* the *sarcophagus of Bishop Ranieri* and the *tomb of Baldassare Coscia, the Antipope John XIII* (1427), designed by Michelozzo and Donatello. The tribune in the apse has Byzantine style *mosaics* on the vault made around 1225 by Fra Jacopo. The entire cupola is covered by other mosaics made between 13th and the 14th centuries by Florentine artists, possibly assisted by Venetian craftsmen. These artists included Cimabue, Coppo di Marcovaldo and Gaddo Gaddi. The tondo above the apse represents *Christ* surrounded by scenes of the *Last Judgement*. The opposite side contains *Stories of the Baptist*, scenes from the *Life of Christ*, and from the *Life of Joseph and Mary* as well as *Stories from Genesis*.

GIOTTO'S CAMPANILE

Begun in 1334 by Giotto, who as *capomastro* was overseer for the construction of the Duomo.

Up to his death in 1337, he built the lower part of the campanile comprised of two enclosed floors decorated with hexagonal and rhomboid *reliefs*, by Andrea Pisano, Luca della Robbia and Alberto Arnoldi.

The relief panels on the lower band, now replaced by copies, represent the *Life of Man* with *Genesis* and *Arts and Industries* (Andrea Pisano and Luca della Robbia to Giotto's designs).

The two upper storeys were carried to completion by Andrea Pisano, who took over from Giotto.

Between 1350 and 1359 Francesco Talenti finished the campanile, adding two levels with two gabled two-light windows with lovely twisted columns and the level with a single three-light opening. On the top, over 81 metres high, he created the large terrace supported by small arches and with an openwork balustrade.

THE MEDICI
a family and their city

The two most famous members of the Medici family:
Cosimo the Elder on the left, and Lorenzo il Magnifico above,
portrayed by Pontormo and Vasari respectively.

Tuscans, and originally from the area of the Mugello, about 1250 the Medici family came to Florence where they were at first merchants in the Wool Guild and later bankers in the Bankers Guild (Arte del Cambio) where they rapidly made their fortune. The first members of the family to settle in the city began their political career rather tentatively and without any great success. However, during the most serious social struggle in the history of the Florentine Republic, the Ciompi Rising (1378), one of those who defended the "lower orders" was Silvestro de' Medici – a supporter of the cause of the wool workers ('ciompi') who demanded representation at the highest levels in the city; this alignment was to provide the foundations that would guarantee the dynasty's prestige amongst the lower classes of society.

But it was with **Giovanni di Bicci** (1360-1429) that the family's power and influence was firmly established. Having accumulated a vast economic fortune as a banker and merchant and also as a result of obtaining a contract to act as the city tax collectors, he contributed generously to the Republic, financing the rebuilding of the church of San Lorenzo, becoming the patron and financier of Masaccio, a standard-bearer in 1421 and in general consolidating democratic and popular support for the family. Giovanni's son, **Cosimo the Elder** (1389-1464), founded the main branch of the Medici family and his descendants were to govern the city through various vicissitudes until 1537. Known as the Pater Patriae, Cosimo emerged victorious from his struggle against the city hierarchies and especially against his rival Rinaldo degli Albizzi. Affirmed by popular support, he became a genuine ruler of the city, exercising his power from a distance having appointed loyal and trustworthy colleagues to the most important offices, and residing in his villas at Careggi and at Cafaggiolo in the Mugello where the dynasty had its origins. He was succeeded by Piero (1414/16-1469) and then by **Lorenzo il Magnifico** (1449-1492) who survived the revolt against the Medici culminating in the Pazzi Conspiracy (1478) in which his brother Giuliano was murdered. Such a glorious political, economic and artistic period flourished within the city and provinces governed by it that Lorenzo's court has been known as the "Florentine Empire". Chased out of Florence when Emperor Charles VIII of France descended on the city in 1494, the Medici returned with the support of the Spanish, and Lorenzo's sons **Giuliano** (1479-1516) and **Giovanni** (1475-1521) the future Pope Leo IX, regained their hegemony. Yet, the Medici no longer enjoyed the full support of the Florentine Republic, deeply affected by the preaching of Savonarola, and in 1527 they were again forced to leave the city. However, with the siege of Florence (1529-1530) by the anti-Republican coalition - lead by the Emperor Charles V - portrayed in a famous fresco by Vasari in the Sala di Clemente VII in Palazzo Vecchio, the Florentine Republic lost its independence and the Medici dynasty was again imposed on the city by Imperial power. The new "Duke of the Florentine Republic" was **Alessandro de' Medici** (1511-1537) who established a tyrannical regime that came to an end in 1537 when he was murdered by Lorenzino de' Medici (*Lorenzaccio*). He was succeeded by **Cosimo the Younger** (1519-1574), son of Giovanni delle Bande Nere, from a minor branch of the family, and Tuscany became a Grand Duchy governed by the Medici until the Lorraine family succeeded in 1737.

PALAZZO VECCHIO

Built as a palace-fortress for the residence of the Priors, the structure was designed by Arnolfo di Cambio in 1294 as a large block crowned by crenellations. The characteristic feature is the powerful thrust of the **Tower** which rises up above the palace and stylistically echoes the upper part. A row of statues is set in front of the building, including a copy of Michelangelo's *David* and *Hercules and Cacus* (1534) by Baccio Bandinelli. Immediately **inside** is the first **courtyard** rebuilt by Michelozzo. Spacious stairs (by Vasari) lead to the **Salone dei Cinquecento**, built by Il Cronaca and decorated by a host of painters chosen by Vasari. Michelangelo's sculpture of *Victory* is on the longer wall to the right. A door at the far right of the entrance leads to the **Studiolo of Francesco I**, the **Tesoretto of Cosimo I** (by Vasari), the **Salone dei Duecento** (1441) by Giuliano and Benedetto da Maiano, and the **State Apartments** which include many rooms with a wealth of paintings and frescoes. A staircase to the second floor leads to the **Quartiere degli Elementi**, by Battista del Tasso and to the **Apartment of Eleonora of Toledo** by Vasari.

A view of the Loggia dei Lanzi and, below, Palazzo Vecchio and Piazza della Signoria.

PIAZZA DELLA SIGNORIA

The political centre of the city from the Middle Ages and still today, this is one of the most lovely squares in Italy. The imposing complex of **Palazzo Vecchio** towers over the piazza. To the right is the lovely **Loggia dei Lanzi**, a late Gothic structure by Benci di Cione and Simone Talenti (1376-82), enlivened by a row of important statues including Cellini's famous **Perseus with the Head of Medusa** (1554), and the **Rape of the Sabines** (1583, the cast of which is in the Accademia) and **Hercules and the Centaur** (1599), both by Giambologna. To the left of the palace is the lively **Fountain of Neptune**, or Fontana di Piazza, by Bartolomeo Ammannati (1563-75) and, to one side, the **Equestrian Monument of Cosimo I** (1594) by Giambologna.

CIMABUE (Cenni di Pepo) (Florence, documented until 1302)

Santa Trinita Madonna

Tempera on wood, 385x223, 1260-1280

Cimabue is regarded as one of the great architects of the modernization of Italian painting and is traditionally believed to be the teacher of Giotto. This Madonna still shows the influence of the Byzantine tradition. There is, however, an unprecedented tension in the profiles and in the attempt to create spatial depth, which is rendered by superimposing the figures and in the concave structure at the base of the throne behind the figures of the prophets Jeremiah, Abraham, David and Isaiah.

THE UFFIZI
the masterpieces

The Palazzo degli Uffizi was commissioned from Giorgio Vasari by Cosimo I de' Medici in 1560, and completed, according to the original project, by Alfonso Parigi and Bernardo Buontalenti in 1580. It was built next to Palazzo Vecchio, following the latter's enlargement, to house the offices of the city magistracy. The palace of the Uffizi is a long, U-shaped structure, almost a theatrical enclosure, which extends as far as the north bank of the Arno. Building it involved sacrificing the glorious old church of **San Piero Scheraggio**, which was partly demolished and partly incorporated into the new edifice. On the ground floor Vasari built lofty arcades supported by alternating Doric columns and pilasters and above them a loggia, which initially had no specific use. It was Cosimo's successor, Francesco I de' Medici, who decided that the loggia should have the present-day function of a gallery, and he commissioned Buontalenti to build the **Tribune**, where the Grand Duke ammassed numerous precious objects and ancient medals. Francesco also set out the first corridor of the gallery, placing in it the Medici family's collection of Greek and Roman statues, from which the *Galleria delle Statue* gets its name.

After Francesco's death, Ferdinando I de' Medici had the classical statues of Villa Medici transferred from Rome to Florence, thus further enriching the collection, to which the finest pieces from the Medici Armoury and a collection of mathematical instruments were also soon added. The Gallery benefited from other substantial acquisitions in the 17th century, notably that of the wife of Ferdinando II de' Medici, Vittoria della Rovere, whose dowry contained the immense patrimony of her grandfather Federico, Duke of Urbino, including precious works by Raphael and Titian. The other important acquisition enriching the Medici collections was Cardinal Leopold's bequest to his nephew Cosimo III de' Medici, who built new rooms in order to accommodate it, and constructed a new and more monumental entrance to the Uffizi. Cosimo's daughter, Anna Maria Ludovica, last of the Medici and widow of the Elector Palatine, added works by German and Flemish masters, and through a family Pact of 1737 settled that the art collections belonging to her family be left to the city of Florence. The **Galleria degli Uffizi** thus became the city's first art museum, a museum that in the following decades continued to grow and inspired the creation of other prestigious Florentine museums.

MICHELANGELO BUONARROTI
(Caprese, 1475 - Rome, 1564)

Holy Family with the Young Saint John, (Tondo Doni)

Tempera on wood, diam. 120
c. 1507

The Tondo Doni (Holy Family with the Young Saint John) was executed on the occasion of the marriage of Agnolo Doni and Maddalena Strozzi, and is the only painting on wood which we know with certainty was by Michelangelo. It is a highly sophisticated work, executed when Michelangelo had only just turned thirty but was already establishing himself as one of the greatest artists of his time. It is remarkable not only for the exceptional technical virtuosity, the thorough knowledge of anatomy, the variety and skill of the composition, but above all for the characterization and vigorous individuality of the figures.

BRONZINO (Agnolo di Cosimo)
(Florence, 1503-1572)

Portrait of Eleonora of Toledo with her Son, Giovanni

Oil on wood, 115x96
c. 1544-1545

The noblewoman is portrayed together with Giovanni, one of the eight children she bore for the Grand Duke. Sumptuous in the stiffness of the precious brocade dress, Eleonora rises before us with an almost architectural majesty. The outline is extremely fine and precise, and the modelling is essential, with no shadows or expressive lines, but only the impassive splendour of her perfectly smooth, alabastrine flesh.

BOTTICELLI (Sandro Filipepi)
(Florence, 1445-1510)

The Birth of Venus

Tempera on wood, 172x278.5, 1484-86

The subject probably derives from Ovid's Metamorphoses and Fasti - where the Hour (or Time) is described in the act of offering Venus her cloak - and therefore from all later humanistic literature.

Primavera (Spring)

Tempera on wood, 203x314, 1482-83

This painting, perhaps Botticelli's most popular and most exploited work, was seen by Vasari in the Villa di Castello of Cosimo I de' Medici. On the right Zephyrus pursues Flora, who, being possessed, scatters flowers over the world; Venus, in the centre, represents Humanitas, for whom the humanists of the Medicean circle reserved great respect; the dancing Graces follow and on the far left Mercury disperses the clouds.

THE GALLERY

The Museum of the Uffizi Gallery has known a period of unbroken development since the 16th century, one marked by successive acquisitions of works and collections. This has involved the progressive enlargement of the space required to house them. Thus, the area of the museum, which in the past occupied only that part named 'The Gallery', was extended to incorporate also part of the Vasari Corridor and the Tribune. In 1988 the rooms of the ground floor and the first floor (originally used as offices of the Signoria) became available following the transferral of the State Archives, hooused in the Uffizi since 1852, to a new site. As part of the **"Nuovi Uffizi"** project, the subsequent triplication of space enables the numerous works kept in the storerooms of the museum to be displayed. In the rooms the paintings and sculptures are arranged chronologically and are displayed in clearly defined sections which correspond to the centuries of their respective production.

Thus it is possible to admire, in succession, the sections dedicated to **Painting of the 13th and 14th century**, the **Painting of the 15th century**, **North European Painting**, the **Tribune**, **Painting of the 16th century** and **Painting of the 17th and 18th century**.

MICHELANGELO'S DAVID

Much of the immense popularity of the Accademia Gallery is due to the statues by Michelangelo housed here – the Prisoners, S. Matthew and especially the David which underwent restoration in 2004. The highly sophisticated procedure made use of the latest techniques in order to preserve intact the patina of the work's 500 year existence and the result has been praised for the delicacy of the operation which preserved a David that is still entirely recognisable to his public. It took months of hard work between 1502 and 1504 for Michelangelo to create his masterpiece in polished marble. David symbolises physical and moral integrity and strength and was originally located in front of Palazzo Vecchio to represent the will to defend the civil and political independence of the Florentine Republic. The biblical character is caught at the instant of greatest tension, anticipating the encounter with his enemy and before, his foot firmly on the head of the vanquished, before he can claim victory over Goliath.

The church of Santa Croce: the façade.

ACCADEMIA GALLERY

Designed like a church with a Latin cross plan, the Gallery houses an extremely important collection of sculpture by Michelangelo. Inside is the original statue of David (1501-1504), recently restored. It is located in the spacious Tribune especially built for it by the architect Emilio de Fabris at the end of the 19th century. In the room that leads to the Tribune, hung with tapestries, is the *Palestrina Pietà*, whose attribution to Michelangelo is controversial, the unfinished *St. Matthew*, made for the Florentine cathedral, and the four *"Prisoners"* (or Slaves), meant for the tomb of Julius II in St. Peter's in Rome, left unfinished, as are these male figures who seem to be trying to free themselves from the grip of marble. Three small rooms are to the right of the Tribune and contain various *shrines* attributed to Bernardo Daddi. To the left is another series of three small rooms containing works by famous masters of the 14th century. Beside the Tribune another large *hall* contains works of the Florentine 15th century. Of special note the new exhibit arrangement for the **Collection of Medicean and Lorenese musical instruments** owned by Conservatorio Musicale L. Cherubini.

BARGELLO MUSEUM

The Bargello palace was built in 1255 as the headquarters of the Capitano del Popolo. The ground floor is occupied by the spacious **Entrance Hall**, the **Courtyard** and the **Room** which contains interesting pieces of 14th-century sculpture. Important works by Michelangelo are housed in the nearby **Sala Michelangelo**, such as *Bacchus* (1496), the *Pitti Tondo* (c. 1504), the *David* or Apollo (1530) and *Brutus* (1540). In the same room there is also a bronze *Bust of Cosimo* by Cellini, and Giambologna's *Mercury*. On the first floor in the room that was once the **Great Council Chamber** are works by Donatello including *St. George* (1416), the young *St. John*, and the bronze *David*.

THE CHURCH OF SANTA CROCE

The church is one of the city's largest and has a neo-Gothic **façade** added in the 19th century. The building, attributed to Arnolfo di Cambio, has a majestic tripartite **interior**. In the **right aisle** is the famous *Madonna del Latte*, a bas-relief by Antonio Rossellino. Along the wall are the *funeral monuments of Michelangelo Buonarroti*, by Vasari (1564), *of Vittorio Alfieri*, poet and patriot, by Canova (1803), and of *Niccolò Machiavelli* by Innocenzo Spinazzi (1787). The church also contains an octagonal pulpit by Benedetto da Maiano (1475); a tabernacle in *pietra serena* with the *Annunciation* by Donatello (1472-76); the *tomb* of the historian *Leonardo Bruni,* by Rossellino; the *funeral monument to Gioachino Rossini* and also one to the poet *Ugo Foscolo* by Antonio Berti (1939). In the **Castellani Chapel** or *Chapel of the Sacrament,* in the right arm of the transept, is the cycle of frescoes by Agnolo Gaddi (1385). Further on, at the head of the transept, is the **Baroncelli Chapel** with the fine fresco of the *Madonna of the Girdle with St. Thomas,* by Bastiano Mainardi (1490) and the cycle of *Scenes from the Life of Mary,* by Taddeo Gaddi; on the altar is the fine *Coronation of the Virgin* by Giotto. Michelozzo's portal in the right side of the transept leads to the **Sacristy**, originally built in the 14th century, and with *Scenes from the Passion* by Niccolò Gerini on the right wall. In the central or east wall of the Sacristy is the **Rinuccini Chapel** with scenes from the *Lives of the Virgin* and of *St. Mary Magdalen* by Giovanni da Milano and a fine *altarpiece* by Giovanni del Biondo (1379).

The church of Santa Croce: the interior.

Various chapels with important works of art open off the back of the central part of the transept: the **Velluti Chapel** with *Scenes from the Legend of St. Michael Archangel*, perhaps by Cimabue; the **Bellacci Chapel** with a lunette-shaped vault with *Scenes from the Life of St. Andrew Apostle* by Giovanni da San Giovanni; the **Silvestri Chapel** with the *monument to Carlotta Buonaparte*, by Lorenzo Bartolini; the **Peruzzi Chapel** with the magnificent *Scenes from the Life of St. John Evangelist* by Giotto (1320); the **Bardi Chapel** with the *Scenes from the Life of St. Francis* by Giotto (1318), followed by the **Cappella Maggiore** (Chancel) with the *Legend of the True Cross* (1380) by Agnolo Gaddi. On the altar is a polyptych with the *Madonna* and *Saints* by Niccolò di Gerini and, above the altar, a *Crucifixion* or Triumphal Cross, of the school of Giotto; next comes the **Tosinghi Chapel** with a *polyptych* by Giovanni del Biondo on the altar; the **Benci Chapel**; the **Ricasoli Chapel**; the **Pulci Chapel**; the **Bardi di Vernio Chapel**. The *tomb* of the humanist *Carlo Marsuppini (1455-58)* by Desiderio da Settignano, and of *Galileo Galilei* (1642) by Foggini are in the left aisle. At the back of the **Cloister** is the marvellous **Pazzi Chapel** decorated inside with glazed ceramic roundels by Luca della Robbia which Brunelleschi designed with a broad, rectangular plan; there are pilasters along the walls and above is a dome with segments, crowned by a lantern. Entrance to the former **Refectory** and the **Museo dell'Opera di Santa Croce** is from the First Cloister.

A moment during the game of football in costume that is played in Piazza Santa Croce.

HISTORIC FOOTBALL

Still highly popular in Florence today, this tournament most certainly dates back to the 15th century when, in 1490, matches were played for three days on ice over the river Arno. Now, three games are played every year towards the end of June. The aim of the game is to get the ball into the opposing team's net and the tournament is played by the teams of four Florentine districts: Santa Croce, Santo Spirito, San Giovanni and Santa Maria Novella.

Each match, between two teams of 27 players, lasts 50 minutes. Hitting the ball with the hands is allowed as it must be constantly in movement and no holds are barred. Frequent fights break out even at a distance from the ball as defenders try to block any attack in advance by totally immobilising their adversaries. An important part of the game is the parade in costume that precedes it, formed by over 500 people elegantly clothed in Renaissance dress.

FLORENCE CITY OF ART

Some of the magnificent works of art that have made Florence renowned throughout the world.

Two famous painted wood crucifixes returned to their original splendour by expert restoration:

Below, a fresco by the mature Giotto, the *Funeral of S. Francis* in the Church of Santa Croce, part of the sequence of *Stories of S. Francis* (Bardi Chapel).

Left, Cimabue's *Crucifix*, in the Church of Santa Croce. Damaged by the flood that hit Florence in 1966, it was for many years the symbol of the city damaged by this dramatic event.

Above, Giotto's *Crucifix* a youthful work by Cimabue's pupil: after lengthy restoration it has been placed in what was probably its original location, above the central aisle of the Church of Santa Maria Novella.

Above, one of the panels made by Lorenzo Ghiberti belonging to the Baptistery "Gates of Paradise", now housed in the Museo dell'Opera del Duomo.

Right, two works in the Bargello Museum which houses the finest examples of Florentine renaissance sculpture: Donatello's *David*, and *Mercury* by Giambologna, both in bronze.

Below, the Brancacci Chapel in the Church of Santa Maria del Carmine: a detail of the *Tribute Money,* perhaps the best known of the splendid frescoes by Masaccio which decorate the chapel and provided a unique point of reference for all Renaissance painting.

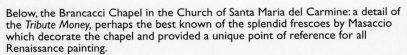

THE CHURCH OF SANTA MARIA NOVELLA

Begun in 1279 by Sisto da Firenze and Ristoro da Campi, it was finished in 1348 by Jacopo Talenti with the campanile in Gothic style (1330). The **façade** was completed between 1456 and 1470 by Leon Battista Alberti, who designed the portal and the part above it divided into compartments by inlaid marble and framed by the coats of arms (sails of fortune) of the Rucellai who commissioned the great work. The **interior** is subdivided into a nave and two aisles by piers carrying pointed vaults. In the second bay of the **right aisle** is the *tomb of the Beata Villana*, by Rossellino (1451), and the **Cappella della Pura**, a Renaissance structure built in honour of a miracle-working *Madonna*, a 14th-century fresco, in the corner to the left. In the right arm of the crossing is the terracotta *bust of St. Antoninus* and, above, the *tomb of Tedice Aliotti, Bishop of Fiesole*, by Tino di Camaino. Steps lead to the **Rucellai Chapel** with remains of frescoes of the *Martyrdom of St. Catherine* by Giuliano Bugiardini; at the centre of the pavement is the fine *tombstone for Leonardo Dati* by Ghiberti (1423). From the crossing there is access to the **Bardi Chapel** and the **Chapel of Filippo Strozzi the Elder** with important frescoes, including scenes from the Lives *of St. Philip and St. John Evangelist* by Filippino Lippi (1503). On the far wall is the *tomb of Filippo Strozzi* by Benedetto da Maiano (1491); the **Chancel (or Cappella Maggiore)**, with frescoes on the vault and on the walls with scenes from the *Lives of St. John the Baptist* (on the right) and of the *Virgin* (on the left) by Domenico Ghirlandaio (late 15th century). Next are the **Gondi Chapel**, decorated by Giuliano da Sangallo, the **Gaddi Chapel** and the **Chapel of the Strozzi family of Mantua**. Masaccio's *Trinity*, an extremely important fresco, is in the **left aisle**; on the second pier is a *pulpit* designed by Brunelleschi. The gate to the left of the façade leads to the Cloisters of the Great Convent: the **First Cloister**, the famous **Spanish Chapel** by Jacopo Talenti (1359), the **Chiostrino dei Morti** (Cloister of the Dead) and the **Chiostro Grande**. A recently-restored *Crucifix* by Giotto adorns the nave.

THE CHURCH OF SAN MINIATO

The lower part of the **façade** is decorated with fine arches; the upper part is simpler and has a fine 12th-century mosaic with *Christ between the Madonna and St. Miniato*. The **inside** is tripartite with a trussed timber ceiling. On the walls are fragments of 13th and 14th-century frescoes. The large **crypt** closed by a *wrought-iron gate* of 1338 is outstanding. Returning from the crypt note should be taken of the raised **Presbytery**, which has a fine *pulpit* (1207) and inlaid wooden *choir stalls*. In the conch of the apse is a large mosaic of *Christ between Mary and St. Miniato* (1277). To the right of the presbytery is the entrance to the **Sacristy**, completely frescoed by Spinello Aretino (1387) with sixteen *Scenes from the Legend of St. Benedict*.

San Miniato, the lovely decorated façade.

Santa Maria Novella: the façade designed by Leon Battista Alberti.

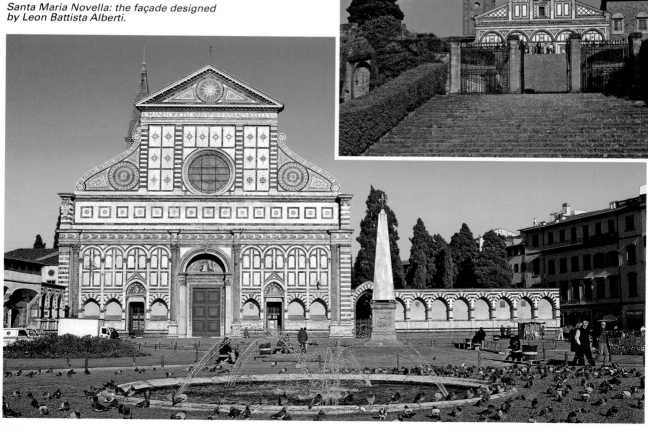

THE CHURCH OF SAN LORENZO

Consecrated by St. Ambrose in 393, San Lorenzo is the oldest church in the city and was rebuilt along Romanesque lines in 1060. The present building dates to 1423 and was designed and built by Brunelleschi. The simple bare **façade** lacks the marble facing: Michelangelo's design was never carried out. The **internal façade,** which Michelangelo also designed, is comprised of three doors between two pilasters with garlands of oak and laurel and a balcony on two Corinthian columns. The **interior** has a nave separated from the side aisles by Corinthian columns. The coffered ceiling has magnificent gilded rosettes on a white ground. The **Sacrestia Vecchia** or Old Sacristy at the back of the left transept was built by Brunelleschi between 1419 and 1428. Earlier than the church, the sacristy is the first example of early Renaissance architecture and of the work of Brunelleschi. The Medici Chapels are the mausoleum of the Medici family and include the **Chapel of the Princes** by Matteo Nigetti and the **New Sacristy** by Michelangelo.

PITTI PALACE

Situated on the Boboli hill, this is the most imposing of the city's palaces and dates to 1457 with design probably by Brunelleschi; in the 16th century the Medicis commissioned Ammannati to enlarge it. Access to the **interior** is through the great portal with its central arch which leads into a charming Doric atrium by Pasquale Poccianti (1850). This leads to Ammannati's famous **courtyard**, at the back of which is the **Grotto of Moses**, carved in porphyry by Raffaele Curradi; antique Roman statues are set under the arcades at the sides, while to the left is the **Museo degli Argenti** and on the right, the **Chapel** frescoed by Ademollo with a magnificent *altar* of inlaid pietra dura and a fine *Crucifix* by Giambologna. The *scalone d'onore,* lined with antique busts, begins on the same side of the courtyard; on the landing is the *Medici Genius* by Giambologna; on the first floor is the vestibule leading to the **Royal Quarters** and the **Palatine Gallery**. On the second floor is the **Galleria d'Arte Moderna**. The portico in the right wing of the façade of the palace leads to the **Bacchus Courtyard** with the *fountain of Bacchus* by Cioli, which portrays the court dwarf of Cosimo I. The courtyard leads to **Boboli Gardens**, the largest monumental green space in Florence.

PALATINE GALLERY

The Palatine Gallery is the second museum of the city, both for size and interest, after the Uffizi, and houses works that are of enormous importance in the history of art. The Gallery was created by Ferdinando II de' Medici.

A view of Palazzo Pitti.

Boboli Garden, the Amphitheatre.

As time passed, the collection - a typically 17th-century picture gallery where the walls are entirely covered with pictures in keeping with the taste of the times - was enlarged by Cardinal Leopoldo de' Medici and, later, by the last members of the Medici and Lorraine families. The visit begins in the **Sala degli Staffieri** and **Statue Gallery** where antique sculptures from Villa Medici in Rome are housed. Exhibited in the Gallery's many rooms are masterpieces such as *La Velata* (Portrait of a Woman) (1514-15), *Madonna and Child and St. John* by Raphael (circa 1516); portraits by Titian, Veronese and Tintoretto; *St. John the Baptist* by Andrea del Sarto (1523); *Madonna and Child with Stories from the Life of St. Anne* by Filippo Lippi (1450). In the early 20th century the Savoy family donated the palace to the nation making it possible to increase the number of works exhibited.

A view from Piazzale Michelangelo.

VIALE DEI COLLI AND PIAZZALE MICHELANGELO

The **Viale dei Colli** winds for about six kilometres around the hills on the south side of the city. It was designed in 1868 by Giuseppe Poggi, the architect who also made the plans for **Piazzale Michelangelo**, an enormous terrace overlooking Florence. In the piazzale are copies of Michelangelo's sculptures: *David* and the four *allegorical figures* on the Medici tombs in the New Sacristy of San Lorenzo.

A reconstruction of the acropolis in Fiesole.

A view of the Roman theatre and surrounding archaeological area.

FIESOLE

This ancient city of Etruscan origin lies at the top of a hill overlooking Florence. The geographic position of the town provided a strategic point for controlling communication routes between central and northern Etruria. The town centres around the lovely **Piazza Mino da Fiesole** with the old **Church of Santa Maria Primerana** and the **Cathedral of St Romolo** built by Bishop Jacopo il Bavaro in 1028 and enlarged in the 13th century. Inside is the important Cappella Salutati, frescoed in the 15th century by Cosimo Rosselli and the *Tomb of Bishop Salutati* by Mino da Fiesole.

The **Palazzo Vescovile** (11th cent.) lies across from the Cathedral. At the top of the hill, built on the remains of the acropolis, is the **Church** and **Franciscan Convent** (14th cent.), which houses the **Ethnographic Mission Museum** containing important Etruscan artefacts. It is a short walk from the piazza to the **Museo Civico Archeologico** and the lovely **Roman Theatre** dating from the first century B.C. where frequent theatre and cinema seasons are held. Nearby are the **Roman Baths** and the **Etrusco-Roman Temple**. Not to be forgotten is the fine **Museo Bandini** which houses sculpture and painting from the 13th to the 15th centuries, and the early Christian **Basilica of San Alessandro**.

VINCI

Of Etruscan origin, Vinci developed around the **castle of the feudal Conti Guidi family** and in the 13th century passed under Florentine dominion. Its appearance today is still that of the 13th century. The town is famous above all as the birthplace of the great genius, **Leonardo da Vinci**. The **Leonardo da Vinci Museum**, opened in 1953, houses one of the largest collections of models, machines and designs invented by Leonardo. The reproductions have been built following precisely his notes and sketches. Over the years the museum has been reorganised and enlarged thanks to contributions from sponsors, scholars, businesses and public and private bodies.

LEONARDO DA VINCI

Leonardo di Ser Piero was born in Vinci on 15 April 1452, the illegitimate son of a well-to-do notary. Even as a young child his ability to learn rapidly and easily and to analyse with sharp logic was quite evident. His artistic training took place in the workshop of Andrea Verrocchio in Florence and he later became a protégé of Lorenzo il Magnifico. Still a young man, however, Leonardo was summonsed to the most important courts and capitals of the day – in 1482 to Milan to the Sforza family, in 1499 to Venice, in 1503 to Florence and later to Rome and again Milan, finally travelling to France on the invitation of King Francis I. Leonardo died at Amboise in France on 2 May 1519. A genial character, he was an extraordinarily gifted painter, architect, scientist and writer.
As a painter, he developed the "sfumato" technique of shading with delicate contrasts of light and shadow, the best example of which is seen in his *Last Supper*.

Leonardo da Vinci, the Annunciation *(1472-75), housed in the Uffizi Gallery in Florence and above, the "Man of Vinci" a wooden structure by Mario Ceroli in the square of the Castle of Vinci.*

PRATO

This important industrial city has a long tradition in the textile sector. Prato has an interesting historical centre and **Piazza del Duomo** is surrounded by old buildings such as the marvellous **Cathedral of S. Stefano** in Romanesque style, dating to the 12th century. The bell tower was designed by Guidetto da Como at the beginning of the 13th century and was completed in 1356-57. Outside the Cathedral is the splendid *Pulpit of the Holy Girdle* (the original panels are in the **Museo dell'Opera del Duomo**), a work by Donatello set on a bronze capital by Michelozzo (1434-38).

Interesting features **inside** the cathedral are the goblet-shaped pulpit (15th century) by Mino da Fiesole and Rossellino (1473); frescoes of the *Stories from the lives of St Stephen and St John the Baptist* decorating the main chapel, by Filippo Lipp and his school (1452-65); *Stories of the Virgin and the Sacred Girdle* (1392-95) by Agnolo Gaddi in the chapel of the Sacred Girdle; and *Stories of the Virgin and St Stephen* in the Chapel of the Assumption, by Paolo Uccello (1397-1475). There are also some important sculptural works such as the *tabernacle of the Madonna dell'Ulivo* (1480) by the brothers Giuliano, Giovanni and Benedetto da Maiano, the *Virgin and Child* by Giovanni Pisano and the *bronze crucifix* on the altar (1653) by Ferdinando Tacca.

In the **Piazza del Comune** are the fine **Palazzo Comunale** and the **Palazzo Pretorio**. The latter houses the **Galleria Comunale** founded in 1850 and recently restored, with its fine collection of paintings, including works by Filippo Lippi, Filippino Lippi, Luca Signorelli and Giovanni da Milano. Of note among the other churches is the **Church of San Francesco** (13th cent.) which contains the *Monument to Inghirami* by Rossellino, the **Basilica of Santa Maria delle Carceri**, by Giuliano da Sangallo (1484-95) and the **Church of San Domenico** (13th cent.). The **Castle of the Emperor**, which dates to the 13th century and was built for the Emperor Frederick II of Swabia.

The large sculpture shaped like a scythe or crescent moon by Mauro Staccioli in the area outside the Pecci Centre in Prato.

An episode from the "Stories of Saint Stephen and Saint John the Baptist" painted by Filippo Lippi in the great chapel of Prato Cathedral.

TEXTILE MUSEUM AND PECCI CENTRE

The **Pecci Centre** (Centro Pecci) is an important and internationally renowned centre for contemporary art. The new **Textile Museum** (Museo del Tessuto) is divided into a Historic Section and a Contemporary Section and is located in the recently restored building of the old Campolmi Factory, a textile workshop on two floors and a splendid example of 19th-century industrial archaeology situated inside the medieval walls of the city.

The Castle of Cafaggiolo.   Opposite page, two aspects of the Villa at Poggio a Caiano.

THE MEDICI VILLAS

Various splendid villas are to be found in the surroundings of Florence. They are existing evidence of the power the Medicis attained and represent a complete territorial system. Sombre and imposing in design, the buildings are vast and impressive. Particular mention must be made of the **Medici Villa of Poggio a Caiano** (1480), built for Lorenzo il Magnifico by Giuliano da Sangallo. The two wings are joined by a hall, a fine portico with piers which runs around the building, and a graceful staircase. The interior contains a wealth of 16th-century frescoes.

Villa Demidoff, originally of late 16th-century design, looks quite different today. A few masterpieces are still to be found in the enormous park (open to the public), such as the *Colossus of the Apennines*, a gigantic statue executed by Giambologna between 1579 and 1580.

Villa La Petraia was once a medieval tower before being transformed into a Medici residence by Bernardo Buontalenti. Important frescoes by Volterrano are inside. The lovely garden contains a *Fountain* by Tribolo and a bronze *sculpture* by Giambologna.

The **Medici Villa of Careggi**, which already belonged to the Medicis as early as 1417, was enlarged by Michelozzo in 1457. The **Medici Villa of Castello**, seat of the Accademia della Crusca, is built along powerful 15th-century lines. There are frescoes by Pontormo and Volterrano inside.

The favourite residence of Lorenzo il Magnifico, the **Medici Castle of Cafaggiolo** was built during the mid 15th century over a 14th-century fortified structure, in the Mugello where the Medici family had its origins. This masterpiece of renaissance art was designed by Michelozzo.

Painted or sculpted, to commemorate an act of patronage or simply of charity, the emblem of the Medici family located on the front of buildings and fortifications indicates the extent of their territorial dominion, yet the significance of the design is still unknown to us. Despite various modifications over time, it always has a series of spheres (usually six) surrounded by an oval frame.

PISTOIA

Pistoia is situated on the northernmost extremity of the fertile plain of the river Ombrone, surrounded by the Arno, Monte Albano and the Apennine slopes. The city's charming small historical centre contains fine examples of architecture. The first inhabitants of the area were Etruscans but not until Roman times did Pistoia begin to take on the characteristics of a town (Pistoriae) reaching its height in the 8th century when it was under Lombard rule. The historical centre is enclosed within the Medici walls built by Cosimo I. In the lovely **Piazza del Duomo** is the **Cathedral** which dates to the 12th-13th century. The beautiful façade has a spacious porch with an important *bas-relief* in glazed terracotta by Andrea della Robbia in the vault. The tripartite interior contains various artistically noteworthy works by artists such as Verrocchio and Lorenzo di Credi. Next to the Cathedral is the **Museo del Tesoro** with interesting examples of gold work and religious furnishings.

Facing the Cathedral is the **Baptistery,** a small octagonal building in black and white marble built to a design by Andrea Pisano in the first half of the 14th century. This lovely building in Gothic style has three finely decorated portals and a gallery of polylobate blind arcading at the top of the wall just below the dome. The lintel of the main portal is sculpted with bas-relief *Stories of St. John the Baptist* and the lunette above contains a *Madonna and Child* with at the sides two fine statues of *St. John the Baptist* and *St. Peter* by the school of Andrea Pisano. Opposite the Baptistery is the bell tower (13th century) built on the remains of an ancient Lombard tower.

Next to the Cathedral is the **Palazzo Comunale** (or Palazzo degli Anziani / *Elders*), dating to the late 13th century, with a Gothic-arched porch on its severe façade. The **Museo Civico** contains important works of art from the 13th to the 15th centuries. Opposite the Palazzo Comunale is the **Palazzo Pretorio** or Podestà, dating to the 14th century, with simple, decisive architecture. Lastly, next to the Cathedral, is the **Palazzo dei Vescovi** (11th cent.) with a lovely Gothic-style façade, and eight pointed and arched openings on the first floor while the second floor has elegant two-light openings.

Other outstanding historical buildings include the **Church of San Giovanni Fuorcivitas** of which only the left side still retains elements of the original Romanesque structure, while the façade is part of a 14th-century enlargement. Inside, the Church contains a fine *Visitation* attributed to Andrea della Robbia, a *polyptych* by Taddeo Gaddi and a *holy water font* by Giovanni Pisano. The Renaissance **Basilica of the Madonna dell'Umiltà** is also quite lovely. The building consists of two rooms: the atrium and an octagonal structure. Mention must also be made of the **Church of San Francesco**, an imposing building in

The dome of the Madonna dell'Umiltà church dominates this view over the roofs of Pistoia.

Gothic style with a Latin-cross interior and frescoes by Lorenzetti (the *Virgin and Child with Angels* is now in the Uffizi in Florence), Puccio Capanna and Lippo Memmi. The **Church of Sant'Andrea** (12th cent.) has a fine portal with a statue of *St. Andrew* in the style of Giovanni Pisano in the lunette. The tripartite interior contains Giovanni's famous *pulpit*. Also meriting attention are the **Ospedale del Ceppo** (13th-14th cent.), the **Church of Santa Maria delle Grazie** (15th cent.), the **Abbey of San Bartolomeo in Pantano** (12th cent.), the **Palazzo dei Capitani del Popolo** (late 13th cent.), and the **Medici Fortress**, a Renaissance structure.

The pulpit by Giovanni Pisano in the church of Sant'Andrea.

Ospedale del Ceppo, a detail of the decorations by the Della Robbia family, for which it is famous.

THE DELLA ROBBIA FRIEZES OF THE OSPEDALE DEL CEPPO

One of the finest works of the Tuscan Renaissance, the coloured decoration in enamelled terracotta of this portico was produced by the Della Robbia workshop. Giovanni della Robbia created some of the roundels (1525-1529) that decorate the arches in blue and white glazed terracotta, following the style of those made by his father Andrea for Brunelleschi's Foundling Hospital (Ospedale degli Innocenti) in Florence. The Della Robbia were a Florentine family of sculptors and potters (15th-17th centuries) and it was in their workshop at the time of the founder, Luca (c.1400–1482) that, although the technique was not invented here, the production of glazed ceramics was developed to a supreme level. The high quality of the enamels used and the application to sculptural works of skills previously only employed in the production of dishes and pots, raised this minor art instead to the level of the fine arts.

Montecatini, a spa resort dating from the early 20th century: the Excelsior and below, the travertine colonnade in the Tettuccio establishment.

MONTECATINI TERME

The town lies in a broad plain at the end of the Val di Nièvole. It is famous for its **spas** and has eight springs of prevalently sulphate-alkaline water, an authentic cure-all for disorders of the liver and the digestive apparatus. Particularly charming is the centre of **Montecatini Alto**, an old village around a castle situated on a hill rising above Montecatini Terme.

Above and bottom, sculptures and mosaics in the Pinocchio Park representing some of the characters in the famous tale by Collodi.

The bronze sculpture at the entrance to the park by Emilio Greco.

COLLODI

This ancient village (late 12th century) lies on the slopes of a hill near Pescia. Nearby are many splendid estates, including **Villa Forti** in Chiari and **Villa Cecchi**, known as the *Guardatoia*, but the finest of all is the imposing **Villa Garzoni** (now Gardi dell'Ardenghesca), built between 1633 and 1662 on the site of a medieval castle in a baroque style typical to Lucca. Behind the villa lies the town of Collodi whose fame is in part due to the fact that the Florentine writer Carlo Lorenzini (1826-90), the author of *Pinocchio*, used the name as his pseudonym. He passed his childhood here in the town where his mother was born. In its labyrinth of lanes, Collodi retains a medieval character, clustered around the **Church** that was founded in the 14th century and the ruins of the **keep**.

Not far from Villa Garzoni, near the **Osteria del Gambero Rosso**, designed by Giovanni Michelucci in 1963, is the **Park of Pinocchio** with the *monument to Pinocchio and the Fairy* by Emilio Greco (1956), the **Piazzetta dei Mosaici** by Venturino Venturi and the **Paese dei Balocchi** (Land of Toys) where Pinocchio's adventures are enacted.

Ever since the **Adventures of Pinocchio** by Carlo Collodi appeared well over a century ago in 1883 this fable, as much a metaphor of life as the story of the most famous wooden puppet ever, has fascinated young and old alike. The wooden hero was made by Geppetto, a village carpenter who, living alone and without children, decided to make a puppet who would be company for him. He quickly realised that the stick of wood could miraculously move and talk like a real little boy, or rather, a real boy in search of trouble. Instead of going to school he sold his spelling book so that he could go to the puppet theatre run by the grumpy Mangiafuoco who, however, became quite fond of him and gave him five gold coins. Slyly tricked by two crooks, the Fox and the Cat who wheedled the money out of him, Pinocchio fell prey to a dizzying series of misadventures which, despite good advice from Jiminy Cricket, the Blue Fairy and the White Blackbird, increasingly lead him into bad ways. After five months of merrymaking with Lampwick in the Land of Toys, where "the holidays begin on 1 January and end on 31 December", Pinocchio comes close to death when swallowed by a huge shark, but he finds Geppetto inside and still alive too. Reunited, father and son swim to their escape by miracle and, finally repentant, Pinocchio awakes one day to discover that he has become a "good boy" a real flesh and blood little boy.

CHIANTI

The region of the Chianti with its gentle hilly countryside is bordered by the basin of the Arno to the south of Florence and that of the Ombrone, north of Siena. The area was already inhabited in the time of the Etruscans and then passed under Roman rule. In the 8th century it became a large feud of the noble Firidolfi family. It afterwards became the object of conquest and contention between Siena and Arezzo first, and later between Siena and Florence. The landscape the Chianti presents its visitors is rich in a hundred different ways: with its roads, unpaved country lanes which retain their charm of long ago, and steep paths that wind up to a villa or a castle, parish church or farm. The Chianti is indeed a blessed land (small churches everywhere with an age-old history) and a land of towers, rich in castles (they can be counted by the dozen) where the atmosphere is still authentically medieval. The most important are Castellina, with fine fortifications and old palaces; Radda, with its 15th-century Palazzo Pretorio; and Greve, with its unique main square.

It is hardly necessary to say that the principal activity in the region of the Chianti is agriculture: an agriculture which produces wine famous throughout the world, the "Chianti Classico Gallo Nero", and an olive oil that is just as prized and which is to be found on the tables of true gourmets. The territory of the Chianti is formed of limestone, sandstone and clay schist. Over half of the territory is covered by tall trees: oaks, chestnuts, ilex (holmoak), firs and in part by the Mediterranean scrub including shrubs, brambles, bushes, hedges and aromatic plants. The other half of the land is cultivated as farmland: large vineyards which cover the hillsides in geometric patterns, extensive olive groves that stretch to the horizon. The wine of this land, known for centuries for its delicious aroma, is the result of a perfect mixture of four types of grapes: Sangiovese and canaiolo (purple grapes), malvasia and trebbiano (white grapes). The result is Chianti Classico, the masterpiece of this generous land which has managed to keep its "flavour" of times past.

THE WINE OF CHIANTI

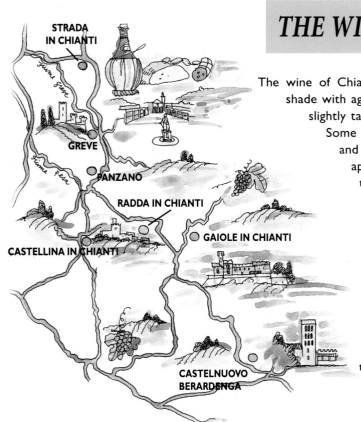

The wine of Chianti is ruby red in colour, tending towards a garnet shade with age, and has a harmonious, dry and full flavour which is slightly tannic, with an intense perfume close to that of violets. Some Chiantis can be drunk young when the wine is fresh and pleasant to the palate, but other areas are known and appreciated for their improvement with medium to long-term aging which matures the singular – even unique – colour, perfume and flavour. Thus there are two kinds of Gallo Nero wines: normal and 'reserve'. The first has a "Gallo Nero" symbol with a red border, while the second has the same symbol with a gold border. Normal Chianti Classico is put on the market on 1 October of the year following its harvest. For a wine to be classed as reserve, however, it must reach 12.5 degrees of alcohol and be aged for a minimum of 27 months at least three of which in the bottle. It is therefore considered an important wine and at harvest time the best grapes are reserved for it.

Tuscan farming traditions of the past: a group photo of the grape harvest in 1933; tools and recipients used in the wine cellars.

Page 36, Badia a Passignano.

A section of 15th-century fortifications at the Castle of Meleto which has given its name to one of the best-known Chianti Classico wines.

The castle of Brolio has medieval origins and is surrounded by imposing ramparts made by Giuliano da Sangallo. The cellars where the Ricasoli age their world-famous wines may be visited on appointment.

The outline of Castellina in Chianti with its characteristic Fortress; right, the medieval street, Via delle Volte.

CASTELLINA IN CHIANTI

High on a hill dominating the Pesa, Elsa and Arbia valleys, set in pleasant countryside dotted with castles and old churches, Castellina is in the heart of a territory that belonged to the historic *Lega del Chianti* (League of Chianti). It developed on the site of one of the oldest Etruscan settlements and was destroyed in the 14th century by the troops of the Duke of Milan, an ally of Siena. The Florentines subsequently built a new ring of *walls* and *fortifications*, most of which have survived, including also a **stronghold** where the town council is now located. The parish church of **San Salvatore** houses an interesting detached fresco of the *Virgin and Child* by the Maestro di Signa and **Palazzo Ugolini** (16th century) is a fine, elegant building, however Castellina in Chianti is particularly noted for the exceptional urban structure preserved almost intact within its walls where there is a network of streets, alleys and arches, typically rural **houses** dating from the 15th -16th centuries and the fascinating, ancient "**Via delle Volte**".

GAIOLE IN CHIANTI

Gaiole was already an important centre in the Middle Ages, thanks to its position: near the route that went from the Chianti to the upper Valdarno; for this reason in the 11th century, all of the markets of the nearby castles moved to Gaiole. The city's fortune regressed only in the last years of the Medici dominion, and in the 18th century, agriculture gave the town news impetus. From an artistic point of view, of interest is the Country **Church of St Maria a Spaltenna,** near the town, built during the first half of the 12th century, although it has been restored during the 18th century. The grand **Castle of Meleto,** a fine example of fortified medieval farmhouse, is situated about two and a half kilometres from Gaiole, towards Siena.

Gaiole in Chianti: the church of Santa Maria a Spaltenna.

A panoramic view of Radda in Chianti with the bell tower in the centre.

GREVE IN CHIANTI

Greve was originally a small country village on the banks of the river Greve, but it soon developed as a result of its convenient position at the junction of important commercial routes that linked Florence, the upper Valdarno, Chianti and the Greve Valley.

The town lies around its large and unmistakable **triangular piazza** where a market has always been held and where a monument has been placed to Giovanni da Verrazzano, the intrepid sailor and discoverer of the bay where New York was founded, who was born in 1485 nearby in the Castle of Verrazzano. Also facing onto this piazza is the interesting **church of Santa Croce**. Beside the little church of San Francesco, in the old Franciscan Convent, is an important **Museum of Sacred Art**. Nearby, the elegant **Uzzano Castle** is certainly worth a visit, as well as the little **San Cresci church**, one of the oldest in Chianti.

Greve in Chianti, the arcades where interesting small shops sell local food specialities and craft items.

Greve in Chianti, the arcaded square.

RADDA IN CHIANTI

Perched high on a hill between the Arbia and Pesa valleys, Radda in Chianti and its ancient castle are surrounded by the thickly wooded hills of Siena. It was a military outpost of Siena until 1176 and then fell under the jurisdiction of Florence. Recognising its vital strategic importance in dominating the distant area of Chianti, Florence assured the town's development by declaring it the chief town of the *Lega del Chianti* and creating an extensive system of fortifications (14th -15th centuries). The new defensive walls enclosed the tow in an elongated oval shape at the centre of which as early as the 15th century, stood the severe **Palazzo del Podestà**. The old **Franciscan convent of Santa Maria al Prato**, soon to house the Museum of Sacred Art, is also of interest. The discovery nearby of the **Poggio La Croce site**, datable to the first millennium BC, indicates that a stable settlement has existed in the area since ancient times.

Siena, panoramic view of the city with the Cathedral and Church of San Domenico.

Siena, Palazzo Pubblico and the 'Mangia' Tower with the Cappella di Piazza, a 14th-century tabernacle.

SIENA

Below, detail of the fresco of Guidoriccio da Fogliano *(1328) portrayed as he leads the Sienese to besiege Montemassi, by Simone Martini in the Palazzo Pubblico.*

On the softly rolling hills of the countryside between the valleys of the Arbia, the Elsa and the Merse lies Siena. The sober and austere beauty of this city with its medieval layout is gradually revealed in all the alleys, small streets, tightly packed houses and airy squares. It is indeed one of the finest examples of a medieval city. Various sporadic finds provide evidence that the area now occupied by the city was already inhabited in the bronze age. An Etruscan settlement seems to have been established on the site of the current town. But the first detailed information dates from Roman times. We, know, for instance, that Siena, at the time *Sena Julia*, must have been a Roman *civitas*, founded as a military colony by Caesar (a legend maintains that the city was founded by Aschio and Senio, Remo's two sons). In the Lombard period Siena was already quite famous. After the was governed by the Bishops until the 11th century when it became a free commune. This was when the city experienced its first great period of territorial and urban expansion, thanks to the flourishing commerce and trade which depended on the route followed by the Via Francigena which linked the city to the area north of the Alps. In the 12th and 13th centuries the city, by now rich and powerful (Sienese bankers used to lend considerable sums to sovereigns, popes and princes), often clashed with the neighbouring city of Florence on which it inflicted a crushing defeat in 1260 in the famous battle of Montaperti. These were also the years in which some of the most important developments in medieval painting took form in Siena. Outstanding personalities such as Duccio da Buoninsegna, Simone Martini and Ambrogio Lorenzetti were active and left inimitable masterpieces, entirely influencing all 14th-century art with their works. In 1269 the Sienese were drastically defeated at Colle Val d'Elsa, this time by the Florentine troops. This signified the beginning of a decline which intensified in the course of the following centuries. In fact in 1487 Siena became a signoria under the control of Pandolfo Petrucci. In the 16th century it allied itself with Charles V and then with Philip II and in 1559 surrendered to the troops of Giangiacomo de' Medici thus passing under the dominion of Cosimo 1. In the centuries that followed it was governed by the Lorraine, as part of the Grand Duchy of Tuscany. In 1859 it was the first Tuscan city annexed to the Kingdom of Italy.

PIAZZA DEL CAMPO AND PALAZZO PUBBLICO

Piazza del Campo, one of the most distinctive squares in Italy, gives the impression of a stage set as it slopes down towards the Palazzo Pubblico in a sort of bowl shape. Most of it is paved in brick and the elegant **Fonte Gaia** stands at the centre of the semi-circle. The lovely reliefs by Jacopo della Quercia, which once decorated the fountain, are now in the Palazzo Pubblico and reproductions have taken their place on the fountain. The

Opposite, the Cathedral of Siena one of the most important examples of Italian Romanesque-gothic architecture.

Palazzo Pubblico, built between the 13th and the 14th century, may well be the most elegant civic building in Italy. The façade consists of a central section (the oldest part) and two perfectly symmetrical and slightly lower wings. The lower part of the structure is in stone and the upper part in brick, all enhanced by fine rows of three-light windows. The interior is a real treasure trove of peerless masterpieces: the rooms on the ground floor (now the Town Hall) contain important *frescoes* by Vecchietta, Simone Martini, Sano di Pietro and Sodoma.

On the first floor one can visit the important **Museo Civico** which has one of the finest art collections in Tuscany. The museum itinerary winds through various rooms, all of which are almost completely covered with frescoes. Works by Spinello Aretino, Parti di Spinello, Jacopo della Quercia, Taddeo di Bartolo, Sodoma, Simone Martini, Vecchietta, and Sano di Pietro can be admired. Two frescoes by Simone Martini, the *Maestà* and *Guidoriccio da Fogliano*, both dating to the first half of the 14th century, are in the **Sala del Mappamondo**. The top floor

houses Etruscan material from the excavations of Murlo.

CATHEDRAL

Dedicated to the Virgin of the Assumption, it is certainly built on the site of an earlier church. Construction began towards the end of the 12th century and work on the Cathedral continued throughout the 13th century. A little after the middle of the century the dome and the first apse of the building were finished, but they were torn down

Above, the monumental Fonte Gaia in Piazza del Campo, once decorated with the original bas-reliefs by Jacopo della Quercia (1409-1419) that are now housed in the Civic Museum.

A detail of the "Effects of Good Government in the City" part of the cycle Allegory of Good and Bad Government *(1337-1339) by Ambrogio Lorenzetti in the Sala dei Nove in Siena's Palazzo Pubblico, the most famous fresco cycle with a secular subject in Sienese painting.*

in the 1320s when Camaino di Crescentino, father of Tino, began the elongation of the apse towards Vallepiatta. In the meanwhile around 1290 Giovanni Pisano had built the lower part of the façade. But before the middle of the 14th century work on the Cathedral came to a halt because the economic and demographic growth of the city, together perhaps with the desire to emulate the great cathedral of its rival Florence, induced the Sienese to plan a church of such a size that the existing building would have served as transept. Lando di Pietro began the construction in 1339, then continued by Giovanni di Agostino and by Domenico di Agostino. But either due to errors in calculations of a static nature, or the change in the economic and political situation, as well as the plague experienced in mid-century, the ambitious project was abandoned in 1355. The **bell tower** is also Romanesque in structure, although lightened by the two-colour marble facing. It seems to have been built on an existent tower of the Bisdomini and is pierced by a series of openings that shift from one-light to six-light as they rise, and is topped

by a pyramid with octagonal base. The Cathedral of Siena houses an incredible number of works of art, which together with those preserved in the adjacent **Museo dell'Opera** provide a complete survey of the artistic culture at its zenith. Among the most important is the **façade** decorated with Giovanni Pisano's *statues,* executed around 1290. Inside, the most striking feature is the marble *pavement,* decorated in sgraffiti or intarsia subdivided into about fifty panels carried out between the middle of the 14th and the middle of the 16th century. A score or so of artists, mostly Sienese, including Domenico di Niccolò and Domenico Beccafumi, had a hand in the work. The *high altar* in the presbytery is by Baldassarre Peruzzi, with the large *ciborium* by Vecchietta; two of the *angels* are by Francesco di Giorgio Martini and others are by Beccafumi. In the left transept, near the area covered by the dome, is the famous octagonal *pulpit* by Nicola Pisano with *Events from the Life of Christ* in the parapet, the scenes separated from each other by *prophets* and *angels.* Executed with the help of Nicolas' son Giovanni, Arnolfo di Cambio, Donato and Lapo di Ricevuto, it must be considered as one of the fundamental developments in Gothic sculpture. In the centuries that followed, the Sienese continued to focus their attention on the Cathedral, as shown by the addition of numerous chapels. Mention must be made of the **Chapel of San Ansano** with the *monument to Cardinal Petroni* by Tino di Camaino and the *tombstone* of Bishop Giovanni Pecci, a bronze by Donatello. The **Chapel of St. John the Baptist** is a Renaissance structure by Giovanni di Stefano, with a bronze *Baptist* by Donatello and *frescoes* by Pinturicchio. The **Chapel of the Sacrament** is also rich in works of art, while the **Chapel of the Madonna del Voto** (or *Chigi Chapel*) was sponsored by Alexander VII shortly after the middle of the 17th century, with the plan by Bernini. To the right of the Cathedral stands what remains of the **Duomo Nuovo**, including the façade, the portal on the right side which leads to the Sabatelli stairs, while in the right aisle the rooms for the **Museo dell'Opera Metropolitana** were obtained by closing off the first three arches. Opposite the steps of the Cathedral is the large complex of the **Spedale di Santa Maria della Scala,** created to care for abandoned children and the poor, the oldest part of which dates from the 9th century. It houses many rare works of art from various periods and is now a centre for cultural exhibitions of a high level.

Siena Cathedral, the recently-restored stained glass window of the choir (1288), made from designs by Duccio di Buoninsegna and dedicated, as is the entire Cathedral, to the Virgin.

Interior of the Cathedral with black and white marble columns.

A detail of the floor of the Cathedral composed of 56 panels, both inlayed and graffito.

THE PICCOLOMINI LIBRARY

The library is just off the fifth arch of the left aisle in the Cathedral and the lunette above the entrance is decorated with a fresco by Pinturicchio depicting the enthronement of Pope Pius III. The pope, whose secular name was Francesco Todeschini Piccolomini, founded the library around 1495. It was intended to house the library of his maternal uncle, Pope Pius II, **Enea Silvio Piccolomini**, the distinguished scholar of humanism who was responsible for the urban remodelling of Corsignano in Pienza, an old fortified village and now one of the best preserved examples of a Renaissance model city, much of which was designed with the help of Leon Battista Alberti and Rossellino. The internal walls of the Library were decorated by Pinturicchio in lively colours with scenes from the life of Enea Silvio Piccolomini. In the centre of the room is a Roman sculpture of the Three Graces. Around the walls, below the frescoes, splendid illuminated choir books are displayed.

Above, a view of Fontebranda in Siena.

church is built slopes sharply down, the large crypt has been installed under the back, as in the church of San Francesco. The **crypt** is divided into a nave and two aisles by robust piers which support the cross vaults. To the right of the church is the 15th-century Cloister. Inside, mention should be made of the *frescoes* by Sodoma in the **Chapel of Saint Catherine**; the *ciborium* and the *angels* on the high altar by Benedetto da Maiano; a detached *fresco* by Pietro Lorenzetti; and works by Matteo di Giovanni, Vanni, Francesco di Giorgio Martini, Sodoma, Casolani, Sano di Pietro, Manetti, while some of the *stained-glass windows* are by modern or contemporary artists.

FONTEBRANDA

In the early 13th century the fountain of **Fontebranda** was installed, representing not only an outstanding example of Gothic architecture, but also constituting the visible part of a complex and innovative subterranean network of aqueducts.

This page and opposite, two works by Duccio di Buoninsegna (Siena c. 1255 – 1318/19), an important innovative force in Sienese painting. Below, Museo dell'Opera Metropolitana in Siena, the Duccio Room: a detail of the Maestà, *surrounded by angels and saints in adoration, the front section of a large altar-piece (1308-11) for the high altar in Siena Cathedral. The reverse side, exhibited in the same room, represents the* 26 episodes of the Passion.

SAINT CATHERINE'S SANCTUARY

The complex developed around the saint's house which was transformed into a sanctuary in 1464. First is the **Oratorio Superiore** (Upper Oratory) with many fine paintings. A small loggia attributed to Baldassarre Peruzzi leads to the **Oratory of the Crucifix**, entirely lined with frescoes, most of which are by Giuseppe Nasini. Turning right at the entrance to the sanctuary the path leads to the **Oratorio della Camera** and the small **cell** where the Saint spent most of her time and where objects which belonged to her are still kept. A small door on the lower floor leads into the **Church of Santa Caterina in Fontebranda**, known also as *Oratorio della Contrada*.

THE CHURCH OF SAN DOMENICO

Begun in the first half of the 13th century, building continued throughout the 14th century and was finally finished after the middle of the 15th century. Since the land on which the

Siena, National Gallery, Duccio di Buoninsegna, the Madonna of the Franciscans.

THE PALIO

Every year the Palio takes place in the Piazza del Campo on July 2nd and on August 16th. In its present form the race dates back to the first half of the 15th century, even though a less spectacular version was run in Siena as early as the 13th century. The event represents an annual renewal of the ancient rivalries between the various districts of the city. Siena is divided into

17 districts, each of them named after a real or imaginary animal: Aquila (eagle), Chiocciola (snail), Onda (wave), Pantera (panther), Selva (rhinoceros and oak), Tartuca (tortoise), Civetta (owl), Leocorno (unicorn), Nicchio (ocean shell), Torre (elephant with tower), Valdimontone (rampant ram), Bruco (caterpillar), Drago (dragon), Giraffa (Giraffe), Istrice (porcupine), Lupa (wolf), Oca (goose).

A procession takes place before the Palio; one after the other the mace-bearers, the standard bearer of the Commune, the trumpeters and palace musicians, the representatives of the five captains, of the 13 districts governed by the podestà and of the 18 vicariates which, in olden times, constituted the Republic of Siena, all file by in order. Next comes the Capitano del Popolo on horseback, followed by the participants of the ten districts which will take part in the race (for every race seven districts are excluded by drawing lots), and finally the wagon carrying the Palio or banner, which is the prize for the winning district. At the tail end of the procession come the ten horses and jockeys who will vie in the race. The horses are lined up near a rope, known as "canapo" and when it is lowered they streak off to circle the piazza three times. The course is almost circular and downhill in stretches and anything but easy for the horses and their riders, but the prize at stake is high and at the end the horse that finishes first will be celebrated for days on end.

The Church of Santa Maria facing onto the main square.

Monteriggioni, aerial view of the village enclosed by the circle of walls and towers.

MONTERIGGIONI

The village clings to a small hillside, enclosed in its impressive circle of **walls**. From a distance the first impression as we glance from one four-sided **tower** to the other (there are fourteen altogether) is that time has stood still and we are in the Middle Ages. The village was built in 1203 by the Sienese who used it as an outpost against the Florentines and as a result of its critical site it often changed hands. The walls went up between 1213 and 1219 and extend for about 570 metres, encircling the tiny, charming village which has a fine **parish church** built in a transitional Romanesque-Gothic style.

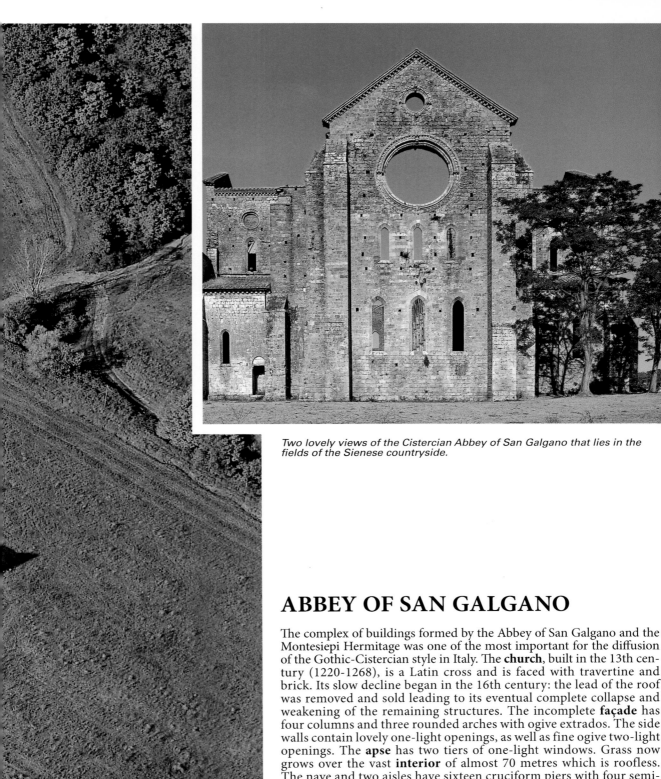

Two lovely views of the Cistercian Abbey of San Galgano that lies in the fields of the Sienese countryside.

ABBEY OF SAN GALGANO

The complex of buildings formed by the Abbey of San Galgano and the Montesiepi Hermitage was one of the most important for the diffusion of the Gothic-Cistercian style in Italy. The **church**, built in the 13th century (1220-1268), is a Latin cross and is faced with travertine and brick. Its slow decline began in the 16th century: the lead of the roof was removed and sold leading to its eventual complete collapse and weakening of the remaining structures. The incomplete **façade** has four columns and three rounded arches with ogive extrados. The side walls contain lovely one-light openings, as well as fine ogive two-light openings. The **apse** has two tiers of one-light windows. Grass now grows over the vast **interior** of almost 70 metres which is roofless. The nave and two aisles have sixteen cruciform piers with four semi-engaged columns. The lovely arches are Gothic with double archivolts. The vaulting of the nave has collapsed. The transept, which is still well preserved, has three aisles with the eastern one transformed into four small chapels. The Cistercian monks had developed an excellent knowledge of the use of symbols and religious geometry in building the Abbey. In fact, some of the analytical research that has been undertaken shows that the geometry is similar to geometrical codes used in the architecture of ancient Egypt. In the **Montesiepi Hermitage** it is still possible to see the *sword in the stone*, the only miracle attributed to San Galgano who is buried in this building.

THE MONTESIEPI HERMITAGE
and the "sword in the stone"

Close by the Abbey of San Galgano, probably previously the site of a pagan cult, is the simple and elegant Romanesque building of the Montesiepi Hermitage. Perfectly circular, it has a vestibule at the entrance and, similar to the Etruscan tumulus tombs, is surmounted by a small dome, the internal vault of which has concentric striped bands of alternating terracotta and travertine. In 1340 a chapel was added, frescoed with *Stories of the Virgin* by Ambrogio Lorenzetti. Exhibited inside in a glass case is the sword that **San Galgano** thrust into the rock so that the hilt would represent a cross (the sword on display is a copy replacing the original which was broken in an attempt to remove it from the rock). This legendary event relates to the life of Galgano Guidotti, born in Chiusdino in 1148, who decided after leading a dissolute life for some twenty years, to join the rule of the Cistercian monks and end his life in prayer and meditation living in a modest hut on Montesiepi. The legend is similar to, and some say precedes, one of the main themes in the myth of King Arthur and the Knights of the Round Table, which was recounted

throughout Europe in the 12th century by bards and minstrels. In the 6th century the problem of succession to the throne of England after King Uther, who had no heirs, was resolved by the magical powers of Merlin who thrust a sword into a stone and stated that only one of the 'elected' could sit on the throne and as proof that the future king was endowed with such nobility of mind, he would be able to miraculously extract the sword from the stone. The young Arthur succeeded and became sovereign of an immense kingdom, carrying out other legendary exploits. The building of the hermitage began immediately after the death of Galgano in 1181 on the spot where his hut had been and in 1185 the Bishop of Volterra consecrated it by decree of Pope Lucius III.

The French order of the Cistercians had great influence in Italy during the 12th century and its most important representatives are seen at the feet of the Virgin in the main fresco of the Chapel of the hermitage: St Bernard of Clairvaux, the most famous exponent of the rule, and St Robert of Molesme who founded the order. In the 13th century, at the foot of Montesiepi the same Cistercian monks who had been responsible for the hermitage built the great Abbey and named it after St Galgano. It is a synthesis of Romanesque elements and of features that belong entirely to French gothic architecture, a splendid example - as is the legend of the saint – of the contacts between the European and Italian cultures during that period.

ARNOLFO DI CAMBIO
(Colle di Val d'Elsa 1245 ca. – Florence 1302)

In the centre of the town of Colle di Val d'Elsa an impressive tower dwelling has been identified as the probable residence of Arnolfo di Cambio and is now known as the Casa di Arnolfo. The birth place of this important sculptor and architect has only recently been known with any certainty, though as an international figure who, during the 14th century, expertly blended

the new influences of French gothic art with classic models, his work has continuously been studied and researched.

The beginnings of his career as a sculptor are well documented, both as an assistant and pupil of Nicola Pisano working on the pulpit of the Cathedral of Siena (1266-68), and when working on the older part of the San Domenico Arch in Bologna (1264-67). During the last twenty years of the 13th century he had his own workshop in Rome where he was influenced by classical sculpture. Several important examples of his work can still be found there such as the ciborium in the church of San Paolo fuori le Mura and the Santa Cecilia ciborium in Trastevere, a lovely combination of architecture and sculpture, the statue of Charles I of Anjou, the statue of Saint Peter in Saint Peter's church, while in nearby Orvieto is the Monument to Cardinal Braye. In 1294 he came to Florence where he designed various buildings including Palazzo Vecchio and the church of Santa Croce and where he died in 1302.

COLLE DI VAL D'ELSA

Famous for the production of crystal and as the birthplace of Arnolfo di Cambio, the town is situated at the centre of an area that was already settled in Etruscan and Roman times. Colle became an independent commune in the 13th century even though it was allied to Florence. In the middle of the 14th century it passed under the domination of Florence and, with the decline of Siena's power, Colle experienced a period of peace and economic prosperity based on industries that exploited the hydraulic energy of the Elsa river. The urban structure of the historic centre of Colle consists of an upper part (**Colle Alto**) and a part that began to develop on the plain in the Middle Ages (**Colle Basso**). The upper part mirrors the lay of the land and stretches out along the ridge of the hill, divided into the clearly separate parts of **Castello** and **Borgo**. Some of the most important monuments in Castello are the unusual Palazzo Campana (1539) and the Cathedral (1603); this small town also has an **Archaeological Museum** in the Palazzo Pretorio and a **Civic Museum** in the Palazzo Priori.

SAN GIMIGNANO

Declared a World Heritage Site by UNESCO, the architecture of San Gimignano makes this small city, so concentrated and noble, unique with the geometric pattern of the towers rising above the town. It was already known in Etruscan and Roman times. During the Middle Ages its importance grew thanks to the presence of the Via Francigena, the most important route at the time connecting Italy to the rest of Europe. San Gimignano almost always sided with Florence, but was unable to expand its power or its boundaries further because geographically it was inhibited by both nearby Florence and Siena.

The two urban spaces with the greatest wealth of art and architecture, are the **Piazza della Cisterna** and Piazza Duomo. The former takes its name from the 13th-century cistern set almost in the centre of the square. All around is a series of medieval buildings including, on the south, the **Palazzo Tortolini Treccani** (14th cent.) with two tiers of two-light windows, the **Casa Salvestrini** and the **Casa Razzi** (13th cent.); on the west side, the twin **Guelph Towers** of the Ardinghelli (13th cent.); and lastly, on the north, the **Palazzo Cortesi** flanked by its **tower** also known as Torre del Diavolo (Devil's Tower).

The **Palazzo del Podestà**, built in 1239 and enlarged about a century later, is situated on **Piazza Duomo**. There is a fine *fresco* by Sodoma on the ground floor. One of the tallest towers (51 m.), the **Torre Rognosa**, rises up over the palace, while opposiste is the **Collegiata**, built around 1239 on the ruins of the old parish church of San Gimignano, with a fine façade in brick and stone. The tripartite Romanesque interior has magnificent cross vaulting. On the internal wall of the façade there are *frescoes* by Taddeo di Bartolo (1393) and Benozzo Gozzoli (1465), and, at the sides, two *wooden statues* by Jacopo della Quercia (1421); on the wall of the right aisle there is a beautiful cycle depicting *Scenes and Episodes of the New Testament* by Barna da Siena. At the back of the aisle is the **Chapel of Santa Fina** (patron saint of the city), with terracottas by Giuliano and Benedetto da Maiano; the frescoes on the side walls with *Episodes from the Life of the Saint* are by Ghirlandaio (1475), the fine *altar piece is* by Giuliano da Maiano. On the wall of the left aisle there is another fresco cycle of *Stories of the Old Testament*. Note the fine *ciborium* (1475) by Benedetto da Maiano on the high altar and an *Annunciation* by Ghirlandaio in the loggia of the *Baptistery*. The **Palazzo del Popolo** (now Town Hall) stands to the left of the Collegiata. It was built in the second half of the 13th century and enlarged in the early decades of the following century. The fine façade is spangled with the coats of arms of the podestà. Inside are the **Museo Civico** and the **Pinacoteca Civica**. The former is installed on the top floor and exhibits extremely interesting works including a fresco of the *Maestà* by Lippo Memmi. The latter contains a valuable collection of paintings of the schools of Siena and Florence from the 13th to the 15th centuries, including works by Filippino Lippi, Coppo di Marcovaldo, Pinturicchio and Benozzo Gozzoli. Near the Piazza del Duomo is the **Piazza Pecori** with the fine **Palazzo della Propositura**, seat of the **Museum of Religious Art** with its rich collection of paintings, precious church furnishings and minor arts. Near the square is the **Rocca**, built by the Florentines in

A view from on high of San Gimignano with its many medieval towers, prestigious symbols that have survived for centuries built by the nobility.

The magnificent outline of San Gimignano.

Piazza della Cisterna.

1353. This solid bastion is pentagonal in plan and has small towers and some remaining walls. Other historical buildings of note include the **Church of San Bartolomeo** (13th cent.), with a brick façade decorated with two orders of blind arches; the **Church of Sant'Agostino** (late 13th cent.), with an extremely simple façade and works by Benozzo Gozzoli, Lippo Memmi and Bartolo di Fredi inside; the **Church of San Pietro** (11th cent.); the **Church of San Jacopo** (13th cent.), with a single nave and unusual elements in the vaults which spring from transverse arches on engaged piers with half columns.

Palazzo del Podestà.

Palazzo del Popolo.

Collegiata di Santa Maria Assunta.

BETWEEN MONTALCINO AND MONTEPULCIANO

THE LAND OF BRUNELLO

The varied scenery of the amazing 'crete' to the south of Siena consists mainly of a land rich in vines, olives and pastures providing produce that is renowned throughout the world. As well as the 'Vino Nobile' of Montepulciano and pecorino from Pienza already mentioned, **Brunello di Montalcino**, supreme amongst single-grape wines, is also produced in the area of the town of Montalcino. The wine originated in the 19th century when Ferruccio Biondi Santi had the innovative idea of concentrating entirely on a single grape and depended on Sangiovese alone (Sangiovese Grosso) to produce a high quality wine – as well as, of course, the climate and soil of Montalcino. The idea was a success and today Brunello is universally recognised, ranking amongst the best wines in the world. Aged in oak for at least 4 years, it reaches 12.5 and 13.5 degrees alcohol; a deep ruby red colour, the taste is dry and lingering, but above all it ages well, and over the years the flavours evolve harmoniously. Bottles produced in good years reach prices that are as heady as the wine itself.

MURLO

S. GIOVANNI D'ASSO

BUONCONVENTO

MONTEPULCIANO

PIENZA

MONTALCINO

S. QUIRICO D'ORCIA

SPEDALETTO

CHIANCIANO TERME

CHIUS

CASTELNUOVO DELL'ABATE

RADICOFANI

S. CASCIANO DEI BAGNI

Barrels of the delicious Brunello di Montalcino wine.

"PICI"

'Pici', a typical pasta of the Val d'Orcia and Siena, are roughly-shaped spaghetti made of wheat flour mixed only with water, and rolled by hand on the pastry board. They should be cooked 'al dente' and eaten with a spicy sauce made of tomatoes well flavoured with much garlic and served with abundant mature pecorino cheese. Alternatively they can be served with "briciole" - crumbs of hard Tuscan bread, gently fried with oil, garlic and hot red pepper.

Panoramic view of Montalcino and the vast 14th-century fortress built by the Sienese for military control of the area.

MONTALCINO

This small medieval city stands on a high plain between the valleys of the Ombrone and the Asso Rivers, and there is evidence of human settlement dating from 30,000 years B.C. The town experienced considerable economic and urban development in the 10th century. In the Middle Ages, both Florence and Siena laid claims to the city and eventually it fell under Medici dominion in 1555. It is famous for the production of "Brunello di Montalcino", a very fine wine for which the city is famous throughout the world.

Of the many buildings in the historical centre which testify to its past, mention must be made of the **Cathedral**, a large structure that was completely rebuilt at the beginning of the 19th century; the **Church of S. Egidio** (14th cent.) which contains a fine fresco of the 15th-century Sienese school; the **Church of Sant'Agostino** (14th cent.) with a simple gabled façade and with various frescoes dating to the 14th century inside; the **Church of San Francesco** (13th cent.); the imposing **Palazzo Comunale** (town hall, 13th-14th cent.); the **Museo Diocesano** (installed inside the Seminary) which boasts a valuable collection, consisting of works by Sienese artists of the 14th and 15th centuries. The **Museo Civico** contains outstanding works by 14th- and 15th-century Tuscan artists. The **Museo Archeologico** houses prehistoric and Etruscan archaeological material found in the area; and lastly, not to be overlooked, is the beautiful **Rocca** or Fortress, built in 1361.

Radicofani, the tower of the old Fortress.

San Quirico d'Orcia, general view of the medieval centre.

A corner of the village of Murlo.

A panoramic view of Pienza.

The façade of Palazzo Piccolomini, a masterpiece by Rossellino.

PIENZA

Pienza is an authentic masterpiece of town planning. It is the ideal model of a large Renaissance city whose development did not depend on the vicissitudes of history. In the 15th century the status of township was conferred by Pope Pius II Piccolomini who was born here. The central square of Pienza is surrounded by the Cathedral, the Bishop's Palace, the Patrician Palace and the Town Hall.
The **Cathedral** was built between 1459 and 1462 to a design by Rossellino. The fine façade in travertine has three portals separated by pilasters flanked by two orders of columns. The airy and light interior has a nave and two aisles and contains works by great artists including Giovanni di Paolo, Matteo di Giovanni, Vecchietta, Sano di Pietro and Rossellino himself.
To the left of the Cathedral is the old **Canons' House** which houses the **Cathedral Museum** with paintings of the Sienese school, goldsmiths' work, illuminated 15th and 16th-century chorales. The fine **Bishop's Palace** rises up next to it with a lovely façade with two tiers of Guelph-cross windows. The **Town Hall** stands opposite the Cathedral. It was rather thoroughly restructured after 1900 and is in travertine with an austere portal above which are four two-light windows. Lastly, to the right of the Cathedral is the splendid **Palazzo Piccolomini**, also by Rossellino and clearly inspired by the Rucellai Palace in Florence. The square building, of rusticated ashlars, has a façade that is articulated by fine two-light windows. The interior, which can be visited, has many rooms which contain important works of art. The courtyard and the hanging gardens (one of the finest examples of the kind) are also particularly lovely.

MONTEPULCIANO

The town was already in existence in Etruscan times, and has remained medieval and Renaissance in appearance (it is built along a narrow chalk ridge and is enclosed by city walls). The **Cathedral** was built between 1592 and 1630 and contains a *Madonna and Child* by Sano di Pietro and various terracottas by the Della Robbias.

The **Church of S. Agostino** is by Michelozzo and the 14th-century church of Sant'Agnese contains a fine 13th-century *crucifix*. In addition to the **Palazzo Comunale** the **Palazzo Neri Orselli** merits mention. Inside is the Museo Civico with a collection of prestigious paintings and sculpture. Montepulciano is also renowned for its "vino nobile", one of the Tuscan wines most appreciated internationally.

A panoramic view of Montepulciano.

LOCAL PRODUCTS

"Montepulciano is the king of all wines", as Francesco Redi's *Bacchus in Tuscany* claimed and while the **"Vino Nobile"** of Montepulciano, produced from a blend of various grapes from vines in the hills between the Orcia and Chiana Valleys (minimum 12,5° and obligatory two years aging), is noted for its excellence, the natural qualities of a simple **pecorino** cheese from nearby Pienza are certainly no less 'noble'. Behind its apparent simplicity, lie incomparable and sophisticated aromas. Made quite simply from the milk of Sardinian sheep that graze freely on the hills, it is stored in wood for a minimum of three months, just as wine is kept in barrels to give it more body, thus absorbing flavours that range from a sharp wine to the tang of seasoned oak. These aromas are in addition to the unusual underlying fragrance that derives from the herbs found in the clay meadows of this area, the 'crete' in the Val d'Orcia and Asciano: calamint, absinthe, watercress, helychrisum, goat's beard…

*Panini assortiti
Olio-Miele
Pecorino di Pienza*

CHIANCIANO

A small town situated amidst the green hills of Tuscany, Chianciano is one of the most important spa towns of Europe. Its history dates from Etruscan times when its beneficial waters were already noted, though it was while under Roman rule that they became famous. Remains of the defensive **walls**, as well as of the medieval **Fortress**, can still be seen in the city; note should also be taken of the **Collegiata of S. Giovanni Battista**, the **Palazzo del Podestà**, the **Palazzo dell'Arcipretura**, seat of the **Museo della Collegiata**. The **Archaeological Water Museum** (Museo Civico Archeologico delle Acque) houses items of the Etruscan, Roman and medieval periods acquired from both private collections and the sites most recently excavated.

Etruscan sarcophagus with the deceased and a winged female spirit (c. 5th century BC) discovered south of Chianciano, and a panoramic view of the town.

The *MADONNA DEL PARTO* by Piero della Francesca

Almost in Umbria, in **Monterchi**, Piero della Francesca (Borgo San Sepolcro 1410/20-1492) painted the Madonna del Parto fresco seen here after expert restoration in 1992/93. The fresco was painted around 1460 for the church of Santa Maria Momentana in the countryside near Monterchi. It was removed from there following the earthquake of 1785 but it was not until 1888 that Piero della Francesca was identified as the painter. The artist from Borgo San Sepolcro probably painted this emblematic pregnant woman in honour of his mother who was born in Monterchi and died in 1459. The heavy figure, standing solemnly framed by a damask curtain held back by two angels represents an image of woman both sacred and profane.

Piero's skill makes this "expectant Madonna" quite unique, for the natural position of the arms and the expression that deliberately alludes to a maternity that is entirely worldly. The subject is based on a religious image that existed until the 4th century AD – the Virgin was also portrayed with a closed book on her pregnant abdomen, the Old Testament – the Word incarnate in the Virgin. However, the Council of Trent (1545-1563) denounced these images as unorthodox and many were destroyed or altered.

AREZZO

A rezzo is the furthest inland of the Tuscan cities, surrounded by small mountain ranges. It is situated at the confluence of four fertile valleys: the Casentino, the Valdichiana, the upper Valdarno, and the upper part of the Valtiberina.

It is believed that the area was already inhabited in Villanovan times, but it was not until the Etruscans arrived that Arezzo rapidly became a flourishing and powerful centre. Together with Volterra, Roselle, Vetulonia and Chiusi it was one of the most important Etruscan cities of the time, and even promised aid to the Latins against the king of Rome, Tarquinius Priscus. In the 5th century B.C. it was already a large Etruscan principality and in later centuries it became one of the most important cities in Italy after Rome. Under Roman domination it continued to prosper until the 1st-2nd century A.D. when as a result of interminable internecine struggles it rapidly declined. In 575 it fell under Lombard rule and then passed to the Franks until it became part of the Marchesate of Tuscany. In the 11th century it became a free commune: a period of renewed energy followed and the city challenged Florentine supremacy over the region until it was finally irremediably defeated by Florence in the battle of Campaldino (1289). Arezzo thus fell under the Florentine sphere of influence, together with many other cities, and subsequently became part of the Grand Duchy of Tuscany under the Medicis and then under the Lorraine family. The centre of the city lies on the slope of a hill. Above, dominating the urban fabric, is the **Piazza del Duomo**, where the Gothic **Cathedral**, begun in 1227 stands. The façade was rebuilt in the early 20th century. Tall piers supporting cross vaulting separate the side aisles from the nave. There is no transept. Magnificent *stained-glass windows* by Guillaume de Marcillat flood the interior with light. In addition the church contains the 14th-century **Cappella Tarlati;** in the left aisle near the Sacristy is a beautiful fresco of the *Magdalen* by Piero della Francesca. Important works dating from the 14th to the 17th century are exhibited in the adjacent **Museo Diocesano**. Near the square is the imposing structure of the **Medici Fortress,** rebuilt in the 16th century by Antonio da Sangallo. This robust star shaped fortification with bastions is characterized by the high escarpment on top of which is a short stretch of wall. Nearby is the **Piazza Grande**, the most picturesque and monumental corner of the city. Buildings dating to the 14th, 15th and 16th centuries face onto the square. The most noteworthy include the fine **Palazzo della Fraternità dei Laici**, a building in Gothic-Renaissance style, designed and for the most part built by Rossellino; the imposing **Palazzo delle Logge** built to designs by Vasari; the medieval **Torre del Lappoli** and **Torre Faggiolana**. Not far off is the striking **Pieve di Santa Maria** (12th-14th cent.), one of the outstanding Romanesque buildings in the entire region. The marvellous façade was clearly inspired by Pisan-Romanesque precedents. The tripartite interior has a fine trussed timber roof. At the back is the entrance to the austere crypt, which lies under the presbytery. Nearby is the **Palazzo Pretorio** (14th-16th cent.) with a façade completely covered by the coats of arms of the Florentine vicars, and the **House** where **Francesco Petrarca** was born. Of note is the **Palazzo dei Priori** (Town Hall), an austere structure in stone with crenellations and two tiers of windows on the façade. Not to be overlooked are the lovely **Church of San Domenico** (13th-14th cent.), an austere Gothic building with a Romanesque portal, and inside a precious *Crucifix* by Cimabue on the high altar and walls lined with *frescoes* by Spinello Aretino; **Vasari's House**, with frescoes mostly by Vasari himself; the **Church of the SS. Annunziata** (15th cent.); the **Church of Badia** (13th cent.); and, above all, the **Church of San Francesco** (13th-14th cent.) which contains Piero della Francesca's marvellous fresco cycle of the *Legend of the True Cross*, recently restored and one of the greatest works of the entire 15th century.

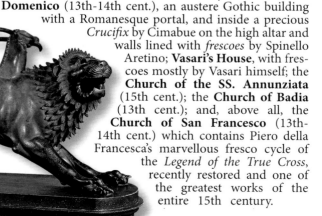

An aerial view of the city showing the church of Santa Maria Assunta.

A view of Arezzo from the Medici Fortress.

The famous "Chimera" of Arezzo, a masterpiece of Etruscan art, housed in the Archaeological Museum, Florence.

The bishop's palace (left) and Palazzo dei Priori, seat of the city council, alongside.

Palazzo Pretorio housing the city library.

A detail of Vasari's loggia flanking Piazza Grande.

Since 1968, stalls of antiques fill Piazza Grande when the Arezzo Antique Fair is held on the first weekend of the month. With some 500 exhibitors from all over Italy it attracts as many as 20-30,000 visitors on each occasion. The first event of its kind in Italy, it was initiated by Ivan Bruschi, an important collector and antiquarian from Arezzo. The Ivan Bruschi Museum, with his collection of over 10,000 items, is now housed in the 14th-century Palazzo del Capitano del Popolo.

CONSTANTINE'S DREAM
by Piero della Francesca

The Church of San Francesco: Piero della Francesca, "Constantine's Dream", is one of the twelve episodes of the famous fresco cycle dedicated to the Legend of the True Cross and now restored. Before his victory over Maxentius in the Battle of Milvian Bridge near Rome, Constantine sees the cross in a dream. Legend has it that it appeared to him with the words "By this sign you shall conquer " and the next morning the emperor ordered the *labarum* to be made – a standard that replaced the Roman eagle with the monogram of Christ's name at the top and under which the soldiers were to fight. Labaro is the name of a Roman village on the Via Flaminia and probably the place where Constantine succeeded in putting his enemy to flight, giving chase as far as the Milvian Bridge. The Roman Emperor thus converted to the new religion and the following year, in 313, he issued the Edict of Milan giving Christians the right to worship freely.

THE JOUST OF THE SARACEN

Reinstated in 1930, this is an old medieval tradition. On the first Sunday in September and penultimate Saturday in June, the four quarters into which the city is divided participate in the famous joust which takes place in the Piazza Grande. The Saracino (a gigantic bust in wood with a steel plaque on his left arm and a long cat-o-nine-tails, to which three leather-covered lead balls are attached, on his right arm) is set up in the north-east corner of the square. Each quarter is represented by a knight who has to strike the plaque with a spear and avoid being hit by the cat-o-nine-tails which in the meantime has begun to spin wildly.

A horseman, his lance at the ready, aims to strike the quintain.

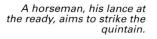

Cortona, Santa Maria delle Grazie, also known as 'Il Calcinaio' and, on the left, the interior.

Below, the façade of the church of San Domenico.

CORTONA

Situated on a splendid natural terrace, overlooking the Val di Chiana below, Cortona is of Etruscan origin and dates from the 4th century B.C. Already famous when an Etruscan city, Cortona became an ally of Rome. In the 13th century it became a free commune but at the end of the century it was occupied by Arezzo. After alternating political vicissitudes the city became a signoria of the Casali family. In 1411 it entered the Florentine sphere of influence and then followed the destiny of the Gran Duchy of Tuscany. The important monuments in the city include the **Cathedral** probably built on the remains of the earlier church of Santa Maria. The building with its austere stone façade was designed and built by the great Giuliano da Sangallo. The tripartite interior was probably also designed by Sangallo even if it was remodelled with a heavy hand in the 18th century. Interesting works of art in the Cathedral include paintings by Cigoli, the school of Signorelli, and by Alessandro Allori.

The **Church of San Francesco** with its simple linear façade and fine portal dates to the first half of the 13th century. The interior contains fine works of art including some by Cigoli, Raffaele Vanni, Pietro da Cortona and Bernardo Radi.

The **Sanctuary of Santa Margherita** dates to 1856. The tripartite interior has various statues of saints on the piers. There is a 13th-century wooden *Crucifix* in the chapel to the right of the presbytery. The earthly remains of Saint Margaret are in a 17th-century silver urn on the high altar.

The **Church of San Domenico**, with its simple ashlar façade and a fine Gothic portal, dates to the early 15th century. The single-nave interior houses outstanding works of art.

The **Palazzo Comunale** is an imposing building dating to the first half of the 13th century. The façade is preceded by a graceful staircase and is surmounted by a solid tower. Inside is the lovely *Sala del Consiglio* with an imposing 16th-century *fireplace*. The **Museo dell'Accademia Etrusca**, in the old **Palazzo Pretorio**, contains an important collection of Etruscan, Roman and Egyptian finds as well as numerous paintings and objects dating from the 13th to the 19th centuries. One of the most interesting examples is a large *bronze lamp* of Etruscan make (5th cent. B.C.).

The **Medici Fortress**, also known as the Girifalco Fortress, dominates the city from the top of the hill. It was built in 1556 by Gabrio Serbelloni and is now used for exhibitions and manifestations.

In the environs of Cortona are to be found the **Church of the Madonna del Calcinaio**, a 16th-century structure, the **Tanella di Pitagora**, which was originally an Etruscan hypogeum (perhaps 4th cent. B.C.), and the **Etruscan Tombs of Camucia**.

Detail of the façade of the Sanctuary of Santa Margherita and the interior.

The polyptych by Lorenzo di Niccolò Gerini which decorates the high altar of the church of San Domenico.

LA VERNA

The sanctuary of Verna is perched on the southern slopes of Monte Penna in the *Natural Park of the Casentino Forests*. In 1213 Count Orlando Cattiani donated the mountain to Saint Francis. The *sanctuary*, surrounded by beech and pine woods, is composed of various buildings: the **Chiesa Maggiore** or **Basilica**, begun in 1348, is a large complex with Della Robbia terracottas inside, including an *Annunciation* and an *Adoration of the Child*; the small **Church of Santa Maria degli Angeli**, dating to the early 13th century, houses a lovely altarpiece of the *Assumption of the Virgin* by Andrea della Robbia; the **Chapel of the Stigmata** is situated on the rock where Saint Francis received the stigmata. Other buildings include the small **Chapel of San Bonaventura**, the **Chapel of Saint Anthony of Padua**, and various **Cloisters**, the whole a marvellous example of sobriety and restraint.

The Sanctuary of La Verna is steeped in natural and artistic beauty as well as recollections of the life of Saint Francis who received the stigmata here.

A view of Chiusi della Verna.

A panoramic view of Poppi and the Castle of the Conti Guidi family, the main monument in the Casentino.

POPPI

Deep in the *Casentino*, Poppi is a medieval town overlooked by the castle of the Conti Guidi (13th century). Its splendid natural and artistic beauty appears untouched by centuries of history; Poppi is within the Natural Park of the Casentino Forest. Within the castle are the Rilliana Library housing medieval manuscripts and incunabula as well as the **Church of the Madonna del Morbo**, begun in 1657 and finished some fifty years later, and the **Church of San Fedele**, an ancient structure dating to 1185-95.

Pisa, a view of the Cathedal with the Leaning Tower in the background.

PISA

Pisa, an ancient Marine Republic, lies 13 kilometres from the sea on a vast flood plain protected on the northeast by Monte Pisano where the lower Valdarno joins the coastal plain. The origins of Pisa are still uncertain even today. Some Latin historians, including Livy, claim that it was founded by the Ligurians. Others, including Servius, maintained that it was built by Phoenician merchants. Whatever the case may be, Pisa does not seem to have fully developed until Roman times when we know it was an ally of Rome in the Second Punic war, a Roman city in 89

B.C. and a flourishing colony at the time of Augustus.

In 641 it fell under Lombard dominion and was strategically important in that it was the first and only port the Lombards controlled until they succeeded in taking possession of Genoa.

Under the Carolingian dynasty it became part of the *marchesato* of Tuscany but, even though a subject city, it was actually sufficiently autonomous to succeed in becoming a free commune at the beginning of the 11th century. This was the beginning of an extremely prosperous period in

its history which lasted almost three centuries. The city became a powerful centre thanks to the control of the seas maintained by its relentless fleet. In this period Pisa became an ally of the Normans and aided them in their conquest of Sicily. It participated in the first crusade with its ships and founded numerous merchant colonies in the East, expanding its commercial dominion. In the 12th century the city was at the height of its fortunes. Pisa won a great victory over the Muslim fleet and later defeated its rival, Amalfi. Evidence of this felicitous period are the many religious and administrative

The Spedale di Santa Chiara, housing the Museo delle Sinopie:
a sinopia from the Stories of Esau and Jacob by Benozzo Gozzoli.

The central aisle of the Cathedral with the marble pulpit
by Giovanni Pisano in the foreground.

buildings which sprang up in the city. Work on the Cathedral was begun and urban growth led to a restructuring of the city walls. Artistically, too, Pisa became a great cultural centre, above all thanks to the genius and personality of sculptors such as Nicola Pisano, his son Giovanni Pisano, and Arnolfo di Cambio, all of whom, together with a goodly group of other illustrious artists, created schools which were so highly regarded that they provided examples throughout Italy.

A slow but inexorable decline began in the 13th and 14th centuries, caused by the continuous clashes on land with its neighbours Lucca and Florence and on sea with its bitter rivals, Genoa and Venice. In the 15th century Florence, ever more powerful, set its eyes on Pisa and after various struggles and vicissitudes Pisa became subject to the Medici city. In addition, the building of the port of Livorno, which in the meantime had gradually become a second and wealthy marine power, deprived Pisa of her supremacy over the seas and definitively sanctioned the city's decline. But Pisa was not a city to be ignored; defeated on a military and political level, it reconfirmed its status as a great city of culture, and one of the most important university centres. In fact it was no less a figure than Galileo Galilei who initiated a prestigious scientific tradition which subsequently continued under the Lorraine dynasty. In 1860 Pisa became part of the Kingdom of Italy. Today, small and self-contained as it is, concentrated around its centre, it is a city rich in cultural activities, stimulated by a flourishing economy that depends above all on the presence of the pharmaceutical, textile and glass industries and by a flow of tourism.

CATHEDRAL

The construction of the Cathedral of Pisa took place predominantly during the second half of the 11th century. The **interior plan** consists of a nave and four aisles, like the largest early Christian basilicas in Rome, but with a projecting three-aisled transept. Women's galleries run along above the side aisles and an octagonal dome is set at the intersection of the nave and transept.

A large apse terminates the nave and also each arm of the transept. Tall columns articulate the nave, interrupted by four piers which support the drum on which the dome rests, while the women's galleries above look out on the nave through broad two-light openings. The interior of this large church is luminous, enlivened by the vivacious polychrome decoration as well as by the play of light and shade which derives from the complex spatial organization. The classic decoration of the capitals in Buscheto's construction (11th-12th cent.) are offset by the decidedly more Romanesque decoration with figures on the capitals that belong to the 12th-century prolongation of the Cathedral.

The outstanding work of art that enriches Pisa's most important religious structure is the *pulpit* made by Giovanni Pisano in the first decade of the 14th century to replace one by Guglielmo which was sent to Cagliari. The pulpit is hexagonal, on a circular base, and is carved with *Stories from the Lives of St. John the Baptist and Christ* in the panels which are divided by figures of *Prophets* and *Saints*. It is one of the finest expressions of Italian Gothic sculpture. There is also a lovely ivory statue of the *Madonna* by Giovanni in the **Cathedral Treasury**. The Cathedral also contains the *tomb of Arrigo VII* by Tino di Camaino. However, it is on the **exterior** that the splendour of multicoloured marbles reaches its zenith. With the exception of the façade, the side walls and the clerestory form an uninterrupted succession of three tiers which encircle the monument. The **façade** also preserves testimony of the principal creators of the cathedral. In the first arch is the *sarcophagus-tomb of Buscheto*; above the central portal on the right, an *inscription* recalls Rainaldo, who began the façade; in the left pilaster, on the level of the pavement, is the *sepulchral inscription of Master Guglielmo*, the sculptor famous for the first pulpit of the Cathedral - a model that continued in use for a long period - and who, with his workshop, finished the upper part of the façade.

THE LEANING TOWER

Pisa's bell tower (also known as the Leaning Tower) was begun in 1174 by Bonanno. At first the tower must simply have sunk down into the ground, but later it began to lean, perhaps as a result of attempts to remove infiltrations of water in the foundations. Therefore in 1185 when the tower had arrived halfway up the third storey the work was interrupted. Building began anew in 1275 under the direction of Giovanni di Simone and in only nine years another three and a half floors were raised. Around the middle of the 14th century Tommaso Pisano was charged with terminating the tower with the present belfry after having levelled off the floor corresponding to the seventh cornice. All these vicissitudes in the construction of the tower did not alter Bonanno's original design, except for the height and the belfry. It is said that inspiration for the circular form of the tower came from Ravenna but it might also have come from the Orient. The decoration is in any case related to the façade of the Cathedral, as is confirmed by the ground floor gallery of blind arches on engaged columns and the floors above with small galleries articulated by cornices. In the late 1950s the movement of the tower had once more slowed up and the difference between the base and the top was then five metres and seventeen centimetres. Before the immense task of consolidation (1990-2001), the overhang had increased by about a millimetre per year.

Aerial view of "Campo dei Miracoli" with the Baptistery, Cathedral, Bell Tower and the Camposanto.

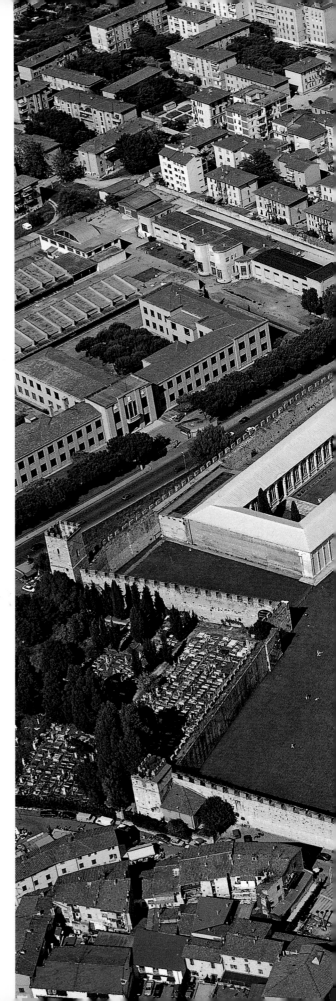

BAPTISTERY

The building was begun in 1152 by Diotisalvi. The ancient chronicler Maragone informs us that in 1164 the columns were set up in only 15 days. In 1260, under the direction of Nicola Pisano, the gallery of small columns was added and the design for the Gothic facing is also his. It must be noted that around the middle of the century the main furnishings for the Baptistery were also in place: the **baptismal font** by Guido da Como in 1246 and Nicola Pisano's **pulpit** in 1260. After the middle of the 14th century the conclusive phase in the construction of the Baptistery went into effect when it was decided to cover the building with a dome.

Although the Baptistery, like the other monuments in Pisa, is based on a two-colour scheme, the most important decorative feature is its sculpture. Examples are the decoration of the portals, especially the main portal which was given a *Madonna* by Giovanni Pisano in the lunette, and the rich decoration of the galleries where the *heads* (now replaced by copies) at the imposts of the arches were mainly by Nicola and Giovanni Pisano. The imposing ground plan of the Baptistery of Pisa is circular and the **interior** consists of an annular nave covered with vaulting which rests on columns and piers. Over the nave there is a women's gallery which faces onto the interior through arcading supported by piers.

THE CAMPOSANTO MONUMENTALE

The Camposanto was begun in 1278 to a design by Giovanni di Simone who, in 1263, had also built the Hospital on the other side of the square. Entirely faced with marble in two delicate shades, the Camposanto consists of a rectangular gallery - the long south side marks the edge of the Piazza - around the field of the old cemetery. **Outside**, the gallery is closed by blind arcading springing from pilaster strips, with sculpted heads at the imposts of the arches.

The internal court of the Camposanto and a view of the monuments in Piazza dei Miracoli.

Inside, the gallery faces onto the field through an arcaded portico on piers and with slender four-light openings. The interior walls of the Camposanto were frescoed, especially in the 14th century, and other tombs were added to those of the illustrious Pisans. At the beginning of the 18th century antique sarcophagi, many of which had been used as tombs in the cathedral grounds, were also transferred here. In the 19th century ancient and medieval material found in the city was brought here so that today the Camposanto is one of the most important museums in Pisa, also for the important fresco cycles it contains.

The north arm of the gallery contains the famous *Scenes of the Old Testament* by Gozzoli, the *Stories of St. Efisio* by Taddeo Gaddi and Spinello Aretino, and further frescoes by Antonio Veneziano and Andrea Bonaiuti. There are also various important sarcophagi of the 2nd-4th centuries A.D. The west arm houses sculpture of the school of Giovanni Pisano such as the *monument to L. Ammannati* (1359) and the *Sepulchre of the Gherardesca* (1315). Also of importance are various Roman sarcophagi. Most of the works of art are in the north arm, including the fine frescoes by Piero di Puccio (1390). Of particular note is the famous **Hall of the Frescoes** with the magnificent *Triumph of Death*, *Universal Judgement* and other frescoes by Buonamico Buffalmacco.

The fresco hall (Salone degli affreschi) in Pisa's Camposanto: details of the "Triumph of Death" and, below, the "Universal Judgement", both 14th century.

Opposite, works in San Matteo National Museum in Pisa: a group of painted crosses (12th and 13th centuries). The various aspects of religious emotion in this period are reflected in the representation of Christ's body, sometimes "triumphant", vital and with the eyes open, and sometimes "patient", mortified.

The Infant Christ in a panel painting by Gentile da Fabriano, Virgin in Adoration *and the* Madonna del Latte *by Nino Pisano.*

S. Sebastian *by Ghirlandaio,* S. Paul *by Masaccio, and the wooden figure of the* Annunciation *by Andrea Pisano.*

Housed in the old Benedictine monastery of San Matteo on Lungarno Mediceo, the museum is considered to be one of the most important in Italy. Conceived as a museum to house works from the local area, it came into being in the 18th century and contains works from the major religious buildings of Pisa and the surrounding area, gifts of noble Pisan families and property acquired by the State from those monasteries that were suppressed after the creation of the Kingdom of Italy. Among the most important works are the collection of Pisan sculptures (14th-15th centuries), paintings of the Pisan and Tuscan schools (12th-14th centuries) and an impressive gallery of Italian and foreign artists (up to the 18th century). The museum also houses masterpieces such as Masaccio's *Saint Paul*, a *Madonna dell'Umiltà* by Gentile da Fabriano and a polyptych by Simone Martini. Pisan sculpture of the 14th century, identified by the innovative style of Nicola and Giovanni Pisano which developed between the end of the 13th and beginning of the 14th centuries, is represented in the museum by works created in their workshop – including a *Nativity* by Tino di Camaino – and the famous *Madonna del Latte* by Andrea and Nino Pisano. The museum also has the largest collection of painted crosses from the 12th to the 13th centuries. Since the last century, the museum has

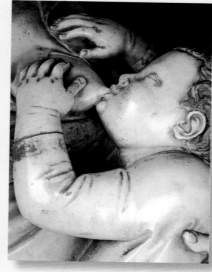

held many exhibitions intended to increase public awareness of the collections it holds. In 1946 an important exhibition of 14th-century Pisan sculpture was held, while following their restoration, works such as frescoes, panels, wood sculptures and ceramic bowls have been displayed, and more recently, in 1995, an exhibition took place illustrating the relationships between medieval Pisa and the world Islamic.

SAN PIERO A GRADO

This majestic basilica in Romanesque style was built between the 10th and 13th centuries on the foundations of a precedent early Christian building. Legend relates that it was here, perhaps driven by a storm, that Saint Peter landed on his way from the Holy Land to Rome. The spacious building is one of the first examples of Pisan Romanesque architecture. The *frescoes* which cover the walls of the nave are attributed to Deodato Orlandi, a painter from Lucca who worked in the basilica at the beginning of the 14th century.

San Piero a Grado, the interior.

San Miniato, a view of this historic town.

San Miniato, the sweeping view from the Fortress.

CERTOSA DI PISA

Founded in 1366, this imposing complex of buildings includes the **Church**, the **Guest House** and the **Cloister**. The entrance vestibule leads into a large square dominated by the **Monastery** with the fine marble façade of the church and two flights of the long staircase at the centre.

SAN MINIATO

Of Etrusco-Roman origin, San Miniato lies along the tops of three hills and most of it stretches out on either side of a single street. The majestic **tower of Frederick** rises up above the houses while further down, the **Cathedral** dominates the town. The **Museo Diocesano** has been opened next to the church and it contains many works from other churches in the diocese. But the religious building which best preserves its original features is probably the **Dominican Church** dedicated to **Saints James and Lucy**, which dates to 1330. Also of interest is the **Palazzo Vescovile**, which overlooks the same square as the Cathedral and which was once the residence of the Capitano delle Milizie and has been a bishop's see since 1622.

VOLTERRA AND THE ETRUSCANS

The earliest references to Volterra date to the iron age and the Villanovan period (9th-7th cent. B.C.). As **Velathri**, it was for a long time one of the most powerful principates in Etruria. It was so important that in the 3rd century B.C. it had approximately 25,000 inhabitants and was the last principate to fall to the Romans after a siege that lasted two years (81-80 B.C.). Towards the end of the 7th century B.C. it developed from existing villages joining up and was positioned on a steep hill with natural terraces from which it was easy to control the surrounding area due to the wide panorama towards Pisa and to the Apuan and Apennine mountains in the north. Volterra developed mainly between the 5th and 4th centuries B.C. as a result of widespread farming activity, alabaster production which even then was well developed, but principally due to the exploitation of the mineral resources of the area. Copper was available from surface seams in Montecastelli, Monterufoli and Micciano in the Cecina Valley and there were other mines between the Era and the Evola as well as at Castellina Marittima, Riparbella and Terriccio. Etruscan Volterra also had an extensive road network for its commercial activity. Goods to be transported by sea could use the naval ports of Populonia and Pisa, while towards the interior they were transported via roads through the Cecina valley, and the Era and Elsa valleys, from where they could link up to the Florentine axis and the Po valley. Via the Etruscan town of Fiesole the minerals extracted were, in fact, even exported beyond the Apennines to Marzabotto and Bologna.

The city was quite powerful between the 12th and 14th centuries when it often found itself fighting Pisa, Florence, Siena and San Gimignano for a question of territory and finally fell to the Florentines in 1361. One of Volterra's most picturesque monumental areas is the Piazza dei Priori, framed by an austere mosaic of palaces: the **Palazzo del Monte Pio**, a solid, elegant building that has recently been restored; **Palazzo Pretorio**, a union of several buildings dating to the 13th century; the **Torre del Podestà**, in the upper part of which a humorous beckoning figure of an animal, baptized by the inhabitants of Volterra the "porcellino" or piglet, stands on a ledge; the **Palazzo Incontri**, seat of the Cassa di Risparmio of Volterra (Savings Bank), in great part rebuilt in period style; and finally the **Palazzo Vescovile** with a unique overhanging roof.

In addition to these is the **Palazzo del Popolo** or dei Priori, the first example of its kind erected in Tuscany. The façade, with many two-light windows and dotted with the polychrome coats of arms of the podestà, is crowned by the pentagonal tower. Open to the public, inside on the first floor is the **Sala del Consiglio**, decorated with a large late 14th-century fresco of the *Annunciation and Saints*, and the **Sala della Giunta** which has a beautiful wooden *ceiling*. The palace contains the civic offices and the **Picture Gallery** (Pinacoteca) with works by Volterrano, Florentine and Sienese artists of the 14th to 17th centuries. The so-called **Porta all'Arco** (4th-1st century B.C.) is set into the Etruscan city walls on the south side of the town, towards the sea. The outer and inner sides of the gate each have a large arch over four metres wide built in dry masonry with blocks of tufa. On the side facing away from the city three heads in dark stone, so weather-worn as to be illegible, have been set into the arch. The **Cathedral** dates to the 12th century although minor 13th-century changes

Aerial view of the historic centre of Volterra.

are also evident. The **façade** is simple, linear, enriched by a finely decorated marble portal and blind arcading in the tympanum. The lovely **interior** consists of a nave and two aisles with columns and an exquisite coffered ceiling of the 16th century. The **Baptistery** is a 13th-century Romanesque building of great architectural interest that stands opposite the Cathedral. It is octagonal in shape. The portal, richly decorated with sculpted heads, leads to an interior that is striking in its spirituality. The large

Rocca-Fortezza rises at the end of the historical centre. The structure consists of two elements that were once separate: the *Old Fort (Rocca Antica* or *femmina)* which dates to 1343 and which rises at one side of the Selci gate, and the *New Fort (Rocca Nuova* or *maschio)* which Lorenzo il Magnifico had built later (between 1472 and 1475). What remains of the imposing **Roman Theatre** dating to the 1st century B.C. lies on the north side of the city. A good part of the *scenae cavea* and the really fine portico are fairly well preserved. The **Baths**, which have mostly disappeared, were near the portico. Among the various museums and collections in the city note should be taken of the **Civic Museum and Gallery**, in the **Palazzo Minucci-Salaini**, a building with a fine Renaissance façade and charming courtyard. Works by many renowned artists are on exhibit, including Luca Signorelli, Taddeo di Bartolo, Neri di Bicci, Ghirlandaio, Volterrano and many others. Works of great interest, mostly from Volterra and its diocese, are

exhibited in the **Museo Diocesano d'Arte Sacra.** Under the portico, at the entrance to the museum, is a collection of objects from the ancient abbey of the Camaldolesi. Among the most outstanding works in the museum: a *Madonna and Child with Angels*, a marble sculpture by Tino da Camaino; a *bust of St. Linus* in glazed terracotta by Giovanni della Robbia; the *Conception*, a splendid panel painting by Taddeo di Bartolo. One of the main attractions in Volterra however is the **Museo Etrusco Guarnacci.** The museum includes a *prehistoric section*; an *Etruscan section*, the most important both in quantity and quality (over 600 funerary urns are included); and lastly the *Roman section*. The **Etruscan necropolises** lie outside the city walls. Excavation is still being carried out in some of them. They include the *necropolis of the Portone*, with chamber tombs of the 6th-5th century B.C.; the *Guerruccia*, now almost destroyed by the landslides of the Balze; the *Guardiola*; the *Marmini* with its two hypogeum tombs; and *San Girolamo*.

There have been frequent landslides in the area known as **Le Balze** to the west of the city, and these are responsible for its present appearance - an enormous chasm that falls away to the plain below.

A section of Volterra's defensive walls showing the Porta all'Arco, an Etruscan structure dating from the 3rd century BC.

A reconstruction of the defensive walls with the Porta all'Arco.

The Roman Theatre in Volterra.

THE SHADOW OF THE EVENING
Guarnacci Etruscan Museum

Originally in the Florentine collection of the Buonarroti family and acquired by Guarnacci around 1750, this slender little bronze found near Volterra was probably a votive figure (2nd century BC). Little more than 50 centimetres, it became the symbol of Volterra and was named the 'Shadow of the Evening' by Gabriele D'Annunzio.

Below, the tomb cover portraying a husband and wife (Urna degli Sposi) *dated 1st century BC.*

Named after Mario Guarnacci, a priest and scholar who augmented the collection of Etruscan artefacts begun by Canon Franceschini in the 18th century, the Etruscan Museum is one of the most important Italian collections of Etruscan antiquities. The collection of funerary urns produced in Volterra between the 4th century BC and the Imperial period represents the main section of the museum. Mostly made of alabaster, the local stone that the Etruscans of Volterra used exclusively for funerary purposes, and in tufa stone, the oldest have sloping covers and geometric decorations, while, from the 3rd century BC, the cover is surmounted by a figure of the deceased, recumbent as if at a banquet. Another important section is the collection of items from the Acropolis of Volterra including numerous ceramics and architectural elements in terracotta. The collection of materials from the oriental period (8th-6th centuries BC) is also of interest and includes a *kyathos* from Monteriggioni and the *funerary stele of Avile Tite*. The *Lorenzini Head* is a masterpiece of Etruscan art dating from the 5th century BC and is the oldest cult statue in marble from central Etruria.

THE TERRACES
("Le Balze")

Natural historic monuments, these terraces are typical of the unusual and evocative landscape of Volterra, recalling the long distant origins of the area. The abundant remains of shell fossils are indications of the time, long ago, that almost half of Tuscany was covered by sea. The former sea beds, siliceous tufa and sandy slopes together formed a rock structure that has been easily affected by erosion from spring and rain waters, leading to the existing formation and to the typical 'carved' appearance of the land here. In antiquity the terraces frequently collapsed, disrupting the geological structure of the area and the landslips have destroyed much of the precious history of Etruscan *Velathri*.

GROSSETO

Grosseto lies in the heart of the Maremma, near the right bank of the Ombrone river which winds its way across this vast plain. It is about ten kilometres from the sea and dates from the late Middle Ages, although Etruscan and Roman remains have been discovered. This prevalently modern city has spread out around the small compact historical centre marked by the old Medici bastions.

As witnessed by an inscription, the **Cathedral** was begun in 1294 and finished early in the 14th century by Sozzo di Pace Rustichini, known also as Sozzo di Rustichino. The Cathedral was probably built on the remains of a Romanesque church, to judge from the pilasters with engaged columns set against the interior façade and the pilaster strips outside on the side walls. The façade, renewed in the 19th century, has three portals and an elegant loggia with a rose window above. The right side has a fine low-relief portal with a splendid sculpture by Cesare Maccari (1800) and, above, two two-light Gothic windows.

The interior has a nave divided from the two aisles by solid compound piers. At the end of still another bay is the apse, semi-circular outside but square inside. Of particular note in the second bay on the left is a fine *baptismal font* by Antonio Ghini (1470-71) and, in the left arm of the transept, a lovely *altarpiece,* also by Ghini, with a splendid *Assumption* (15th cent.) by Matteo di Giovanni.

The **Museo Archeologico e d'Arte della Maremma,** created thanks to a generous donation to the town of Grosseto by Canon Giovanni Chelli, has a rich collection of art and archaeology. The *Prehistoric section* is installed on the ground floor with material from the Palaeolithic to the Villanovan periods. The *Etruscan section* presents material from the excavations of ancient settlements including Talamone, Vetulonia, Cosa, Sovana, Castro, Vulci, Pitigliano, Saturnia, Magliano and above all **Roselle**, where excavations are still under way in the ancient urban area. The upper floor contains the *Topographical section* displaying the materials according to the river basin where it was found (Ombrone, Fiora, etc.). There is also a rich *Collection of religious art* of the Museo Diocesano of Grosseto on the second floor. Paintings of the Sienese school dating from the 13th to the 17th century include in particular a magnificent *Last Judgement* by Guido da Siena or his circle; a charming *Madonna and Child* by Segna di Bonaventura; a goodly number of works that can be ascribed to the circle of one of the above masters; a moving *Crucifixion* (first half of the 13th cent.) which is of such high quality that the name of Simone Martini comes to mind; the famous *Madonna of the Cherries* by Sassetta; and the two *Saints,* once panels of a polyptych, by Sano di Pietro. The collection also contains works by many other illustrious masters such as Girolamo di Benvenuto, Pietro di Domenico, Riccio, Vanni and Rutilio Manetti as well as a fine **collection of ceramics**.

The austere 13th-century **Church of San Francesco,** in Gothic style, was dedicated by the Benedictines to S. Francis who landed in one of the Maremma ports on returning from the East. The gabled brick façade is enlivened by a portal with lunette and a fine rose window. The convent buildings were on the left side.

Two views of Piazza Dante in Grosseto.

Opposite, the façade of the old San Lorenzo Cathedral.

Still extant is a Cloister with the so-called *well of the "bufala"*, built by Ferdinando I towards the end of the 16th century. Another well lies outside the church opposite the hospital. San Francesco has a single large nave with a trussed timber roof and a fine end chapel. It contains a valuable *cross painted* set behind the high altar, perhaps an early work by Duccio di Buoninsegna (1289) and a lovely wooden *crucifix* (15th cent.) of the Sienese school. The interior is partially decorated with frescoes.

The **Medici Walls** were built in the second half of the 16th century and comprise a powerful bastioned circle of walls. At the beginning of the 19th century the bastions began to be transformed into public gardens and at one corner rises the **Medici Fortress** which incorporates the old **Sienese Keep** (a solid structure consisting of two distinct but interconnected parts with strongly escarped bases bordered by a string course). A fine view of the old town can be had from the fortress.

93

MASSA MARITTIMA

This lovely town clinging to a hill high above the open plain has much interesting evidence of its past in the historical centre. The town is now divided into the "old city" above and the "new city" further below, consisting mainly of modern buildings. Massa Marittima is probably of Etruscan origin but it became really important in the 9th century when it was chosen as a bishop's seat. In the Middle Ages it was one of the most flourishing free communes, thanks to the exploitation of copper and silver mines nearby.

The city **Cathedral** is a lovely building in Romanesque style. Dating to the first half of the 13th century, it was then enlarged in the area around the presbytery and the apse between 1287 and 1304. The splendid façade has seven blind arches in the lower part decorated with roundels. Travertine columns with Corinthian or composite capitals decorated with leaves or figures of animals divide the **interior** into a nave and two aisles. It contains various outstanding works of art. The sculptures near to the main door are evidence of the Lombard period and include one of the *Slaughter of the Innocents* in a quite primitive but very dramatic style. The influence of Lombard art resulted from the presence of Germans who came to seek minerals and primary materials during the Middle Ages and contributed to the development of mining around Massa.

The Romanesque-Gothic **Church of Sant'Agostino** dates to the early 14th century. The bare façade is in travertine and has a solid doorway with a finely decorated rose window above. Next to the façade is the **Cloister** and the square campanile which dates to 1627. The interior with a single nave contains outstanding works of art by Lorenzo Lippi, Rutilio Manetti, and Jacopo da Empoli. The **Church of San Francesco**, part of a monastery that houses the diocesan seminary as established by a city council decree in

An elegant synthesis of Romanesque and gothic architecture, the Cathedral of Massa Marittima, dedicated to S. Cerbone, is raised and set in an oblique position to the square in front, a feature that is a unique characteristic of the town.

Cathedral, interior, the sarcophagus of S. Cerbone, a masterpiece by the Sienese sculptor Goro di Gregorio dated 1324, with 8 sculpted scenes of legends from the life of the Saint. According to tradition, S. Cerbone landed at Baratti in the 6th century and converted the population along the Mediterranean coast to Christianity.

Cathedral, interior, detail of a pre-Romanesque bas-relief.

1524, was built in Gothic style in the 13th century by St. Francis himself. The only part of the original structure left today is the polygonal apse. Once the residence of the Podestà, today the **Palazzo Pretorio** houses public offices. This solid austere building in travertine dates to the first half of the 13th century. The two upper floors are articulated by a row of two-light windows which enliven and illuminate the structure. The **Palazzo Comunale**, an imposing Romanesque building in travertine, has a fine series of two-light windows arranged in three floors. The building, which dates to the 13th-14th century, is actually the result of the fusion of several medieval tower-houses. Among the other monuments of interest mention must be made of the imposing **Sienese Fortress** built around 1335; the **Palazzo Vescovile**, completely rebuilt in 1814; the lovely **House of the counts of Biserno**, a fine Romanesque structure; the **Palazzo dell'Abbondanza**, which dates to the late 13th century; the **Archaeological Museum** with its interesting material from Etruscan tombs; and the **Museum of Mineralogy**.

The "Maestà" by Ambrogio Lorenzetti (1335-37), Palazzo Pretorio.

95

THE MAREMMA

This was once a fertile land where many powerful Etruscan cities stood. The area extends from southern Tuscany as far as north-western Lazio and is divided into **Maremma pisana** and **Maremma grossetana**. Towards the interior it stretches over the western slopes of the Colline Metallifere for a total area of around 5000 square kilometres. Along the beautiful coast are many well-known sea resorts such as **San Vincenzo, Follonica, Marina di Grosseto, Punta Ala, Castiglion della Pescaia** and **Porto Santo Stefano**.

Typical to this area is the figure of the **Buttero**: his job is to drive herds of cattle along difficult and tortuous roads, brand the various herds of cattle and break in the famous Maremma horses (an ancient breed).

The **Natural Park of the Maremma** (also known as the *Uccellina Park*) covers more than 100 square kilometres on the Tyrrhenian coast stretching from Principina a Mare to Alberese and down to Talamone. This is a splendid natural setting where the unspoilt hills become beaches and cliffs crossing through pine groves, cultivated fields, pasture land and swamps.

The Uccellina Park: views of the coast, the wildlife and the marshland, an outing in canoe towards the mouth of the Ombrone.

Next page:
Uccellina Park, a sweeping panoramic view from the Castelmarino tower.

A beautiful scenery in the countryside around Grosseto.

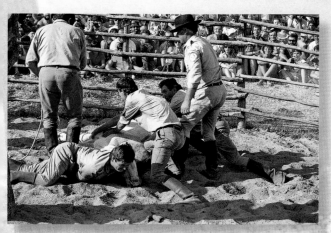

Images of animals grazing and the 'butteri' – horsemen who protect herds living in the wild – involved in branding, capturing and marking the calves with a firebrand. This unique event in the Maremma is a kind of 'rodeo' that has become part of the agricultural traditions in this area of Tuscany.

A variety of important ecosystems characterise the countryside formed by the Uccellina hills, the pine woods of Marina di Alberese, at the mouth of the Ombrone river and the swamp land around Trappola. Further north, the area between Viareggio and Livorno became the **Natural Park of Migliarino, San Rossore, Massaciuccoli** in 1979 and covers an area of 24,000 square kilometres with woods, undeveloped coastal areas, estates, rivers, lakes, marsh and agricultural land. The different kinds of terrain with their varying microclimates has given rise to habitation for a great variety of animals.

THE ETRUSCANS
in the Maremma

The Maremma is one of the areas originally occupied by the Etruscans and some of their most flourishing cities rose here. A stable occupation of the area dates to the early iron age and can be explained by the presence here of both forests and minerals, and by the conformation of the area both on the coasts and in the interior. The small clusters of villages gradually developed until they became small cities which exploited the potential of local resources and created an important flow of trade crossing Etruria during the 7th century B.C. But it was as sea-faring cities that they really flourished, for at the time the coast of the Maremma had many more inlets than it does today. In addition to the large **Bay of Baratti**, which is still a magnificent protected sheet of water, there used to be a vast internal marine lagoon, the **Prile Lake**, onto which both Roselle and Vetulonia faced, and which then became a swamp. It has now been reclaimed and is part of the Plain of Grosseto. Maritime links with the Island of Elba and the other coastal cities of Etruscan Lazio are witnessed by finds relating to trade. From these it can be deduced that these cities flourished as long as the Etruscans maintained their supremacy over the seas, in other words until 474 B.C., when the Syracusan fleet defeated the Etruscans in the waters of Cumae. Some of the cities made a comeback between the 4th and 3rd centuries B.C., a period in which the Roman presence began to extend, although without resistance. The founding in 273 B.C. of Cosa, a Roman colony to be used as port of call, led in fact to the further decline of some of the ports and heralded the gradual Romanization of the area. Various museums provide evidence of the area's heritage of mining and minerals including the **Museum of Iron and Cast Iron** (Museo del Ferro e della Ghisa) in Follonica and the **Mineral Museum** (Museo del Minerale) in Campiglia Marittima, while near San Vincenzo is the **Archaeological-Mining Park of S. Silvestro** (Parco archeologico-minerario di S. Silvestro) which illustrates three thousand years of mining activity. In the area around Campiglia is the important **Archaeological Nature Park of Baratti-Populonia** with artfacts from the Iron Age to Roman times and including the Etruscan necropolis of **San Cerbone**, part of the larger area of the **Val di Cornia** Cultural Park.

An example of an Attic red-figured bowl.

Opposite page, two funerary urns, one painted and with a pitched covering, the other with a figure of the deceased, and a fine ornamental item cast in metal, a reminder that the civilization developed in an area rich in minerals.

The elegant "Baratti Amphora", made of 132 silver medallions decorated with relief figures and housed in the Archaeological Museum of Populonia.

Three ceramic vases in the Maremma Museum of Art and Archaeology in Grosseto.

The Bay of Baratti and view of a necropolis at Populonia.

POPULONIA

The ancient Pupluna was the only Etruscan city situated on the sea. The port, located in the **Bay of Baratti** below the promontory on which the city stood, was already a centre for exchange and trade in Villanovan times. Subsequently, with the exploitation of the iron mines on the island of Elba, the economy of the city reached considerable heights. The oldest necropolises of Populonia are located on opposite sides of the gulf, at **Poggio delle Granate** and at S. Cerbone, and might indicate the earlier presence of two distinct villages which were later fused into the original nucleus of the Etruscan city. The tombs of the period (9th-8th cent. B.C.) are the classic shaft tombs (*a pozzetto*); as time passed the tombs became architecturally more evolved and with richer and more abundant tomb furnishings. In the oriental period (7th cent. B.C.) there was a radical change in the types of funeral structures which tended to be more monumental, as witnessed by the chamber tombs of the **Costone della Fredda** and of the **Porcareccia**, but above all by the imposing tumuli of **S. Cerbone**. Among the most important of the funerary monuments, mention must be made of the **Tomb of the Chariots** (dei Carri), the most imposing in the necropolis of S. Cerbone. This tomb, marked by a large cylindrical drum constructed in blocks of stone, and with stone slabs to carry off the rain water, is topped by a large tumulus of earth. It contained the remains of two war chariots with bronze and iron fittings, gold work, objects in ivory, and bronze and iron arms which date the burial to around the middle of the 7th century B.C. Other tombs in the necropolis of S. Cerbone include the **Tomb of the Cylindrical Pyxides**, the **Tomb of the Balsamario, Tomb of the Pyriform Aryballos** which can be dated to between the middle of the 7th and beginning of the 6th century B.C. Not far off is the **Tomb of the Bronzetto di Offerente** (late 6th cent. B.C.) an aedicule tomb, with a gabled roof. It was surrounded by a series of sarcophagi in the open air, which had already been plundered in antiquity, as is the case with most of the other tombs, and which date to the 5th century B.C. On the **Poggio della Porcareccia**, between the slopes of the town and S. Cerbone, are the **Tomb of the Oreficerie** (gold work), with personal ornaments in gold and silver, and the **Tomb of the Flabelli**, discovered intact, with jewellery, three magnificent fans in repoussé bronze, arms, helmets and a large quantity of bronze receptacles as well as Greek and local pottery. A building was excavated near these tombs. It had several rooms and may have been a centre for the industrial processing of metal, active from the end of the 6th century B.C. to late Etruscan times. Unfortunately a lack of evidence makes it impossible to define the precise location and extension of *Pupluna* in its earliest phase, but presumably the inhabited area was situated where the town and castle now stand. **City walls** about 2,500 metres long defended the town and some sections built with large squared blocks can still be seen. These date to the archaic phase (6th-5th cent. B.C.) when *Pupluna* had become a fully-fledged city, rich and powerful.

VETULONIA

Remains of the imposing Etruscan **ring of walls**, constructed with enormous blocks of stone, can be seen in the medieval part of the town. The excavations of the urban centre of Hellenistic-Roman times are just outside modern Vetulonia, at the **Costa Murata** and along the road that leads to the Aurelia. These paved streets, houses and shops, built in line with a well defined town plan with a sewage system, pavements, basins and wells, date to the Etrusco-Roman period. But only the extensive necropolises can furnish an exact idea of the wealth and power of this centre, from the 8th century B.C. on, when the copper, silver, and lead mines in the Colline Metallifere began to be exploited. The tombs of the archaic period, situated in the heights surrounding the city (**Poggio alla Guardia**, **Colle Baroncio**, **Poggio alle Birbe**, etc.) have rendered many objects in decorated bronze and locally made gold and silver jewellery, as well as precious handmade objects imported from the eastern Mediterranean area, Phoenicia, Egypt, Sardinia. Some of the richest tombs, both in the quality and quantity of the objects contained, include the **Circolo dei Monili**, **Bes**, the **Pellicce**, the **Lebeti**, the **Trident**, and the **Tomb of the Littore**, dating to the late 8th- mid-7th century B.C. In the second half of the 6th century B.C. the monumental tumulus tombs of the nobility make their appearance, with square chambers and false vaulting supported by a central pier: two superb examples along the **Via dei Sepolcri** are the Tomb of the Pietrera and the Tomb of the Diavolino. The **Tumulus of the Pietrera** measures over 60 metres in diameter and has a long entrance corridor to the central chamber where various limestone statues of weeping women and male figures were found. On the slopes of the tumulus several pit tombs were brought to light. The precious objects they contained dated them to the same period (mid-7th century B.C.) as the main sepulchre. Not far off is the **Tumulus of the Diavolino**, of the same period, which takes its name from an animalesque figure engraved on a stone next to the left jamb of the doorway. This sepulchre too, with its large tumulus defined by the drum in blocks of stone, has a false vault which was supported in the centre by the pier of which only the base is still extant. The following centuries have not left many traces, but a few recent finds seem to indicate that life in Vetulonia continued uninterrupted throughout the 6th and 5th centuries B.C., blossoming into a new period of prosperity in the 3rd century B.C.

Vetulonia, ossuaries from the Villanovan period (9th-7th century BC) and a view of the village.

THE TEMPLE OF TINIA

The site of Etruscan Tlamu was identified in 1888 on the nearby hill of Talamonaccio. Just a few years later, in 1892-93, the remains of a pagan temple built during the second half of the 4th century BC were discovered. The temple was dedicated to the god Tinia (or Tin), the greatest Etruscan deity, corresponding to the Roman Jupiter, and was built in the Italo-Etruscan style, with wooden columns and roof, located on the south-east side of the hill, standing on a tufa base. The façade faced towards the sea. Probably about 150 BC a triangular pediment (above) was added, clearly influenced by Greek architecture with terracotta friezes illustrating the saga of the "Seven against Thebes". The pediment was recently restored by the National Archaeological Museum of Florence. The theme is taken from the famous tragedy by Aeschylus *Seven against Thebes* (467 BC) which is derived from Greek mythology and relates the internecine war between the sons of Oedipus, Eteocles and Polynices for possession of Thebes of the Seven Gates: six commanders and their armies each took a gate of the city by storm in order to depose Eteocles and place Polynices on the throne of the city; the conquest of the seventh gate was to be decided by a duel between the two brothers who, however, killed each other.

TALAMONE

Once an Etruscan city, then a simple fishing village, the town is now a flourishing seaside resort. The houses are huddled together on a promontory which dominates the sea. Of particular interest is the 16th-century **Rocca** or Fortress which was probably built to a design by Vecchietta, and the remains of the **Etruscan temple** of Talamonaccio. Mention of the town is made in history books, for in 1860 Garibaldi and his Thousand stopped here to replenish themselves with arms before leaving for Marsala.

Aerial view of the Talamone peninsula between the hills of the Uccellina Park on the left and the bay on the right.

ROSELLE

The excavations of the Etruscan and Roman city of Roselle can be visited. They lie only a few kilometres from Grosseto. The town, set on two low hills divided by a valley, is surrounded by a **circuit of walls** over three kilometres long which has been miraculously preserved in its entirety from the 6th century B.C. until now. Various entrance gates along the wall provide access to the city and entrance to the excavations is through the **East Gate**. The road leads to the heart of the Roman city, then to the **Forum**, with broad streets in volcanic stone, on either side of which are the most important public buildings such as the **Basilica**, with a rectangular ground plan and portico, used for the administration of justice. The paving in stone slabs of the Forum of Roman Imperial times still exists opposite. Further south is what is thought to have been the seat of the *Augustales*, a room with niches in the walls, which contained the marble statues of the emperor Claudius, Livia and other personages of the Julio-Claudian dynasty, evidence of the cult of the imperial family. Protected by modern shed roofs, the remains of various **Etruscan houses** from the archaic period can be seen under the Roman level. Portions of the walls and floors in pressed clay dating to the 7th-6th century B.C. are still extant. On the slopes of the north hill, not far from the road that leads to the excavations, is a **Roman bath establishment** with mosaic pavements and the base of a **medieval tower**, while near the top of the hill are other **Etruscan buildings** of the archaic period and the **Roman amphitheatre** of the first century A.D. with four entrances corresponding to the four cardinal points. On the south hill, excavation has brought to light a vast **inhabited centre** with streets, houses and artisan workshops of the late 6th century B.C., over which lies a later urban settlement of the Hellenistic period.

For a clear correct interpretation of the excavations of the city and of the necropolises, the artistic production and the economy of Roselle, one would do well to visit the permanent exhibition in the Museo Archeologico of Grosseto.

For a clear and correct interpretation of the excavations of the city and of the necropolises, the artistic production and the economy of Roselle, one would do well to visit the permanent exhibition in the **Museo Archeologico e d'Arte della Maremma** of Grosseto.

Above, Roselle, an interesting aerial view of the ruins where the remains of the Roman amphitheatre can be made out.

A stretch of the ancient road.

A small egret rests in the oasis of the Orbetello Lagoon, one of the 80 protected areas managed by the Italian WWF.

THE WWF OASIS AT ORBETELLO

Located in the natural environment of the Giannella sand bar the oasis covers approximately 1500 hectares and is situated on one of the most important migratory routes. One of the main wintering locations for birds that nest in Europe, it gives shelter to about 200 species of aquatic birds including coots, ducks, herons and flamingos. The Oasis was the first protected area for birds to be created in Italy and dates from 1971 when it was discovered that in the west of the Orbetello Lagoon many and often rare species of migratory birds nested, and in particular the **stilt plover,** a wader that had not nested in the Italian marshland for about a century.

.

ORBETELLO

The town is at the centre of the lagoon of Orbetello, which is about 27 kilometres square, with two strips of sand known as *tomboli*. An artificial dam, built in 1842, joins it to the promontory of the Argentario. A visit to Orbetello can begin with the **Porta Medina Coeli**, which was part of the old circuit of walls. The gate leads into Piazza Quattro Novembre, surrounded by the **Spanish fortifications** from the period when it was part of the Spanish garrisons: these fine examples of military architecture were begun by Philip II and continued by Philip III in the 17th century. The 14th-century **Cathedral** is also lovely, although it was remodelled in the 17th century. Inside is a fine marble *altarpiece* of pre-Romanesque art.

The **Palazzo della Pretura** houses the **Antiquarium,** a museum with archaeological material from Etruscan and Roman times from the surrounding territory. Particular attention should be paid to the archaic *sphinx* of the 7th-6th century B.C., various amphorae and finely made sculptures.

A section of Etruscan walls in the town of Orbetello and, below, a panoramic view of the town, situated on an isthmus that links Mount Argentario to the mainland.

A view of the Argentario coast.

ARGENTARIO

This large promontory stretches twelve kilometres out into the sea. It was originally an island but became linked to the mainland by an accumulation of sand which formed part of the isthmus where Orbetello is situated as well as two sandy cordons (*tomboli*) at the sides of the isthmus thus joining it to the mainland and creating the lagoon of Orbetello. It was once an island and became joined to the continent as sand accumulated to form an isthmus. Later, two stretches of sand joined the isthmus to the mainland, creating the Lagoon of Orbetello. On the north this magnificent stretch of land, which juts out into the sea, slopes down into a lovely bay where Porto Santo Stefano is situated.

PORTO ERCOLE

This picturesque coastal town and seaside resort lies on the east coast of the Argentario. The old part of the town clusters around charming streets and small squares where various fine buildings are to be noted: the distinguished **Palazzo Consani** (once seat of the Spanish governor), the **Parish Church**, in which Caravaggio was buried; the spacious **Villa Corsini** with a lovely park that is not unlike a botanical garden with a wealth of rare plants. Dominating the houses from above is the large complex of the **Rocca** with the forts of **Santa Barbara**, **Monte Filippo** and **Stella**, all built by the Spaniards.

PORTO SANTO STEFANO

This well known seaside resort was almost entirely destroyed in World War II and has been fully rebuilt. Now a flourishing port (with the **Porto Vecchio** and the **Porto Nuovo**) it has a large fishing fleet. In the town itself note should be taken of the **Church of Santo Stefano**, built in the 17th century but completely reconstructed after the war, and, above the town, the old bare **Rocca** or fortress. The small picturesque streets are the chief attraction of this pleasant tranquil town.

SATURNIA

This small town lies surrounded by a ring of walls built by the Sienese in 1461 on what was left of the preceding walls thought to be Etruscan. It is known mostly for the **springs** of sulphurous water useful in curing ailments of the respiratory system and of a rheumatologic nature. A visit to the **Etruscan necropolis** a few kilometres from the inhabited centre is quite interesting. There are numerous tombs in slabs of travertine.

SORANO

The town owes its origins to the Etruscans who densely settled the entire area. In the vicinity is the **Etruscan necropolis of Sovana**, excavated at the beginning of the century, with numerous chamber tombs dating to the 4th-3rd century B.C. They are cut into the tufa walls of the cliff that was created by the Calesina and its tributaries. The most interesting is perhaps the **Tomba Ildebranda**, of the 2nd century B.C., in the shape of a temple with columns and capitals in the form of human heads. But the Sorano we see now is that of the Middle Ages, when it belonged to the Aldobrandeschi and then to the Orsini, before becoming part of the Medici grand duchy. The main square contains the **parish church**, remodelled in the 18th century. The **Rocca degli Orsini** or fortress, built in the 15th century and later enlarged, is also imposing. The coats of arms of the Aldobrandeschi and the Orsini recall times past. One can enjoy an extensive panorama from here.

A fascinating view of the cascades at Saturnia's hot springs, where the sulphurous waters flow at a temperature of about 37° C. and are noted for their many therapeutic properties.

Sorano: a crag fortified in the 18th century, the 'Sasso Leopoldino' overlooks the Mediterranean vegetation.

Sorano, the impressive Orsini Fortress, with the Medici coat of arms.

PITIGLIANO

Originally an important Etruscan, and later, Roman city, the town now has a historical centre of characteristically medieval origins. Particularly striking is the **Cathedral** with a fine Baroque façade and numerous important works inside. Also worthy of note are the 14th-century **Palazzo Orsini**, modified in the 16th century by Giuliano da Sangallo, and the simple **Church of Santa Maria** with a late Renaissance façade and a tripartite interior with various fine works of art.

AMIATA

Amiata is the highest mountain peak in Tuscany (1738 m.) and is quite outstanding from a naturalistic point of view. The mountain is of volcanic origin and dates to the Quaternary period. Small streams and springs abound and is a winter sport station. Towns such as **Abbadia San Salvatore**, **Piancastagnaio**, **Santa Fiora**, **Arcidosso**, **Castel del Piano** all have beautiful, ancient buildings and are noted as quite lovely small towns and villages.

A view of Amiata.

The intriguing profile of Pitigliano, built along a rocky ridge of tufa as are many villages in this area. There are numerous caves in the sheer cliff sides that long ago served as burial chambers and now house the fine wines of Pitigliano.

LIVORNO

ivorno is an important sea port the origins of which are uncertain. Probably the area where the city lies was already inhabited in Neolithic times, as evidenced by various finds, but the real birth of the city is relatively recent. After Pisa fell to the Florentines (1405), Livorno passed under Genoa which a few years later ceded it to Florence for 100,000 florins. This was the beginning of the city's prosperity. The population quadrupled and it rapidly became a very important port and the large **Porto Mediceo** was built - a fine structure which added lustre to the city. The city's **Cathedral** was built at the end of the 16th century to a design by Alessandro Pieroni, and was later en-larged in the 18th century. The simple **façade** is entirely faced with marble. The Latin-cross interior has a nave only and contains various fine *monumental tombs* such as the one dedicated to the Marchese Marco Alessandro del Borro and Count Ginori. The **Church of the Conception** is by Pieroni (1599). The façade is simple and restrained. The single-nave interior contains fine works of art including a bronze Crucifix, perhaps by Ferdinando Tacca, on the first altar to the right. The **Museo Civico Giovanni Fattori** is situated in the centre of the park of Villa Mimbelli. It was founded at the end of the 19th century when it was decided to install the numerous collections donated to the city by Enrico Chiellini.

The **Fortezza Vecchia** (in the area of the old port) was built by Antonio da Sangallo the Elder between 1521 and 1534. The director of works was the engineer Nicolao da Pietrasanta. Inside the fort is the small **Church of San Francesco** (mid 16th century) with a chapel alongside (late 17th century) as well as archaeological material from the old Roman castrum.

The **Monument of the Four Moors** by Giovanni Bandini, also known as Giovanni dell'Opera as he was a marble work-er for the cathedral of Santa Maria del Fiore in Florence, is situated in Piazza Giuseppe Micheli and was dedicated to the Grand Duke Ferdinando de' Medici in 1596.

A map of the city of Livorno in the 17th century in a print of the time.

An aerial view of the city and its port.

Two of the four 'Mori', the four bronze statues by Pietro Tacca around the base of the monument to Grand Duke Ferdinand I, in Piazza Micheli.

GIOVANNI FATTORI CIVIC MUSEUM

The Red Tower *by Giovanni Fattori.*

The three storeys of Villa Mimbelli in Via San Jacopo in Acquaviva have recently been restored and now house the traditional civic collection, entirely reorganised according to strict art-historic criteria, as well as a group of works that had for long been kept in storage. In addition to the paintings of Fattori that form the central section of the gallery, works by Silvestro Lega, Cesare and Giovanni Bartolena, Vittorio Corcos, Michele Gordigiani, Leonetto Cappiello, Plinio Novellini and Oscar Ghiglia are displayed. The museum came into being at the end of the 19th century when it was decided to organise the archaeological and numismatic collection donated to the city of Livorno by Enrico Chiellini. The works of Enrico Pollastrini were added to this and in particular a considerable group of paintings by Giovanni Fattori (Livorno 1825-Florence 1908), the most authoritative of the "macchiaioli" painters. Amongst his works here are the Cavalry Charge, Montebello, Roman Countryside *and* Portrait of his Third Wife.

The "Amerigo Vespucci" naval school of the Naval Academy, Livorno.

THE NAVAL ACADEMY

Founded in 1881 by Benedetto Brin, a General of Naval Engineering who designed some of the finest ships of the day and became Minister for the Navy in 1876, the Naval Academy is an authoritative institution that contributes much to the fame of Livorno. The school teaches military engineering and is equipped with laboratories for the study of physics and other sciences as well as a specialized library of over 20,000 volumes. In particular the school is renowned for one of its school ships used for teaching marine skills to young trainee officers, the **Amerigo Vespucci**, one of the most lovely sailing ships in existence that still travels the seas around the entire world. Launched in 1931 from the docks at Castellammare di Stabia, it has a sail surface of over 3,000 square metres and a crew of about 400.

The Four Moors, masterpieces by Pietro Tacca, an outstanding sculptor who worked at length for the prestigious Medici family, were not added until 1626.

The large **Medici Port** begins at Piazza Micheli, continues along the street named Via del Molo Mediceo, where the old **Fortino della Sassaia** is situated, and ends at the wharf known as the **Molo di Cosimo**. On the other side of the wharf is an enormous basin with a large dam called the **Curvilinea**. Further north is the **Marzocco Dam**. Lastly, between the wharf and the curvilinear dam, which is built on rocks, the lovely 14th-century **Lighthouse Tower** rises towards the sky.

Above and below, two views of the Fortezza Vecchia (Old Fort). A large 16th-century fortified complex designed by Antonio da Sangallo for Cardinal Giulio de' Medici (the future Pope Clement VII).

The belvedere on Terrazza Mascagni named after the famous composer who was born in Livorno.

A monument to Francesco Domenico Guerrazzi, born in Livorno and a member of the triumvirate that governed Tuscany during the uprisings of 1848-49.

THE TUSCAN ARCHIPELAGO

Legend recounts that emerging from the water, the Tyrrhenian Venus dropped seven pearls from her necklace and they became *the islands of the Tuscan Archipelago* (Capraia, Elba, Giannutri, Giglio, Gorgona, Montecristo and Pianosa). The beauty of their coasts and the sea (already renowned in the Palaeolithic period) is now protected by the *National Park of the Tuscan Archipelago.*

Views of three villages on Elba: from above, San Piero in Campo, Marina di Campo and Marciana.

ELBA

Elba was already known by the Greeks who had discovered the immense deposits of iron. Later it was occupied by the Etruscans and then the Romans who left outstanding signs of their presence in the form of splendid villas and towns and village which still exist, such as Pomonte and Capoliveri *(Caput Liberum).*

After various vicissitudes in which the island passed first to the Medicis, then was contested by Spain and France, Elba was occupied by the English and three years later fell to the French. From 1814 to 1815 it was independent and Napoleon spent his period of

exile here. It was then annexed to the Grand Duchy of Tuscany and in 1860 to the Kingdom of Italy.

Portoferraio is the chief town of the island; it has a small intimate historical centre enclosed in a powerful 16th-century fortification. It is the principal port in Elba and also a noted tourist resort. Of the fine historical buildings in the centre, mention should be made of the 16th-century **parish church** and the **Town Hall**, which houses the **Biblioteca Comunale Foresiana**. Note also the **Church of the SS. Sacramento** with the *Madonna of the Assumption* by Giovanni Camillo Sagrestani on the ceiling; the **Church of the Misericordia** and the **Forte della Stella**. Other towns and villages on the island include **Capoliveri**, **Porto Azzurro, Rio Marina, Cavo, Marciana** and **Marciana Marina, Poggio** and **Marina di Campo**.

An aerial view of the island of Elba showing the promontory of Cape Enfola with Portoferraio behind, and below, the port of Marciana Marina.

Portoferraio, the historic capital of Elba, the ancient origins of which date back to the Palaeolithic era. The prehistoric town walls made of blocks of granite are evidence of later settlement.

Left, a view of Porto Azzurro.

The village of Capoliveri on the slopes of Mount Calamita: one of the oldest inhabited centres, it is located in a dramatic position overlooking the sea and is in an archaeological area where many items from Roman times have been found relating to the mining of magnetite.

A view of Giglio Castello and, below, Giglio Porto.

GIGLIO

Once occupied by the Etruscans as documented by the remains of a ship that was wrecked in the waters of Giglio Porto, the **Villa of the Enobarbi** in the Castellari area dates, however, to Roman times. The remains of other Roman buildings have been found near Giglio Castello.

The brief journey from Giglio Porto to Giglio Castello (about six kilometres) is one of the most breathtaking experiences available to a tourist in the entire Tuscan archipelago. From **Giglio Porto**, a small centre clustered around its bay, the road rises steeply in the midst of terraced vineyards to the imposing **Torre del Lazzeretto** and further on the **Faro Vecchio**. After a series of curves the austere brooding town of **Giglio Castello** appears ahead, completely enclosed in the grey medieval walls with their round and rectangular towers, and a 14th-century **Fortress** at the summit. The asphalt road which joins Giglio Porto to Giglio Castello has a single fork leading to **Campese**, a tiny village which is the paradise of scuba divers thanks to its limpid water and the variety of fish. Next to the village is the **Torre del Campese** built during the reign of Francesco I, grand duke of Tuscany.

LUCCA

Lucca was founded on a flood plain that stretches from the last foothills of the Tusco-Emilian Apennines to the northern uplands of Monte Pisano, not far from the river Serchio. This ancient and noble city has a wealth of churches and picturesque towers from the time of the communes, Renaissance palaces and fascinating streets. The oldest part of the city is enclosed in the circle of walls which are still in good condition and which give the city its characteristic appearance. In Roman times it was an important *municipium;* the city was then taken by the Goths and subsequently by the Lombards and the Carolingians. In 1119 Lucca succeeded in becoming a free commune and its period of prosperity began. The **Cathedral** stands in Piazza San Martino. It was built in the 12th century in Romanesque style, but was completely remodelled in the 14th and 15th centuries. Three large arches of different size, resting on composite columns, form the lower part of the façade, which is still Romanesque, while above these there are three tiers of loggias. The tripartite interior has important works of art such as the famous *Tomb of Ilaria del Carretto* and the statue of *St. John the Evangelist,* both by Jacopo della Quercia, as well as works by Tintoretto (Last Supper), Civitali (funerary monuments to Pietro Da Noceto and Domenico Bertini) and Ghirlandaio (Virgin and Child with Saints). The **Treasure of the Opera del Duomo**, composed of a great number of religious objects in gold and silver dating to the 14th-15th centuries, is located inside the complex.

Nearby are the **Baptistery**, a small 14th-century building with a square ground plan and a Gothic dome; the **Church of San Giovanni** (12th cent.), considerably modified in the 17th century; the **Monument to Maria Louisa of Bourbon** (1834); the **Palazzo della Provincia**, an unfinished work by

Lucca, an aerial view of the historic centre with the church of San Michele in Foro in the foreground.

Below left, the tomb of Ilaria del Carretto by Jacopo della Quercia (1408), housed in the Cathedral.

Ammannati. **Palazzo Mansi** (17th cent.) is situated in Via Galli Tassi. It contains many magnificent richly-furnished rooms, including the lovely *Camera degli Sposi,* an 18th-century alcove with carving in baroque style. The palace houses the **Palazzo Mansi National Museum** with works by artists ranging from the Renaissance to the 19th century, such as Luca Giordano, Bronzino, Salvatore Rosa, Veronese, Tintoretto and many others.

Nearby stands the Renaissance **Church of San Paolino**, with important 15th- and 16th-century works. Not far off is the imposing silhouette of the **Palazzo Pretorio**, begun in 1492 by Civitali, and the lovely **Church of San Michele in Foro** (12th-14th cent.), an example of pure Pisan-Luccan Romanesque architecture. The splendid façade has four tiers of loggias and the tripartite interior has a perfectly round apse. The church contains notable works of art by Andrea della Robbia, Filippino Lippi and Raffaello da Montelupo.

Another striking religious building is the **Basilica of San Frediano** (12th-14th cent.) with a fine tripartite façade enhanced by a mosaic of the *Ascension* (the Luccan school of Berlinghieri). The interior is divided into three aisles and contains works by Civitale and Jacopo della Quercia. **Piazza dell'Anfiteatro** lies in

Above and below, two
views of Lucca Cathedral.

(meaning built outside the city walls), a fine example of Pisan Romanesque with an essentially linear façade in marble with arcading and loggias.

Also worth visiting are **Palazzo Bernardini**, and the lovely **Villa Guinigi**, which houses the **Villa Guinigi National Museum** divided into two main sections: archaeology (Etruscan, Roman and Ligurian items) and art (including sculpture, paintings and the minor arts). Lastly, the most fascinating feature of the city are its **walls**, built between the 16th and 18th centuries. They stretch for about five kilometres and are still completely intact.

front of the church and is one of the most attractive in the city. It is characterized by the fact that it stands on the site of a Roman amphitheatre of the second century A.D. The **Church of San Pietro Somaldi** (13th cent.) has a fine façade in Pisan Romanesque style and a unique bell tower in brick. Turning into Via Guini are two rows of brick buildings, known as **Case Guinigi** with a tower which is topped by a hanging garden. Further ahead is the 13th-century **Church of Santa Maria Forisportam**

VERSILIA

A famous tourist area on the Tuscan coast since the early 1900s. Amongst the towns here are **Viareggio** which is not only an important resort, but also has an active fishing port and ship yard, and **Forte dei Marmi**, the most elegant tourist centre of the Versilia coast and one of the most famous holiday resorts in Italy.

Views of the beach at Versilia and D'Annunzio during a visit to the Apuan Alps. The writer was often a guest at Villa La Versiliana where the "Versiliana Festival", one of the most important cultural events in Tuscany now takes place.

TORRE DEL LAGO
and Giacomo Puccini

The small town, situated between the Massaciuccoli lake and the Tyrrhenian sea, became famous in the early 1900s due to the presence of the composer **Giacomo Puccini** (1858-1924), who was born in Lucca and built his residence on the shores of the lake. The **villa** of the composer lies only a few metres from the water and contains musical and hunting mementos of the master in the shady rooms, furnished in the Art Nouveau style then in fashion. The statue in the small square overlooking the lake is dedicated to Puccini. Every summer in Torre del Lago there is an interesting musical event, the *Puccini Festival*, during which the great composer's most famous operas are performed, from *La Bohème* to *Tosca*, from *Madame Butterfly* to *Turandot*. The **Puccini Festival** began in 1930 at the express wish of the composer who intended his operas to be enjoyed in the incredible setting of the Massaciuccoli lake.

The statue of Giacomo Puccini on the lakeside walk at Massaciuccoli.

Carnival floats on the seafront in Viareggio.

A poster from the museum of La Scala in Milan.

Manon Lescaut

MVSICA DI G. PVCCINI

MASSA-CARRARA

MASSA

Situated on one of the low hills which lie below the narrow valley of the Frigido river, at the foot of the Apuan Alps, Massa is about five kilometres from the sea. The city contains various interesting examples of medieval and Renaissance architecture although its origins are undoubtedly Roman. Important buildings in Massa include the **Palazzo Cybo Malaspina**, which was begun in 1557 on what remained of an earlier villa of the Malaspina family; the **Cathedral** dedicated to SS Peter and Francis of Assisi, originally 13th-century but heavily remodelled and restored in the course of time; and the **Museo Diocesano**, housed in the old Bishop's Palace. Note should also be taken of the 18th-century **Church of the Carmine** and the **Malaspina Castle**, which consists of a large complex including the **Rocca Malaspiniana** which dominates the entire city, as well as the fortress, built between the 15th and 16th centuries.

CARRARA

Mentioned in Dante's Divine Comedy, the river Carrione flows through Carrara, standing between the sea and the magnificent scenery of the Apuan Alps. Noted for the quarrying and working of marble since Roman times, this is one of the oldest communes in Italy and the town centre reveals various layers of history. The **Marble Museum** exhibits samples of the various types of marble to be found in the Apuan Alps. The **Palazzo Cybo Malaspina** with its 16th-century layout, is the seat of the **Accademia delle Belle Arti**. Next to the **fountain of Andrea Doria,** or the *Giant*, a lovely unfinished work by Baccio Bandinelli, is the **Cathedral**, begun in the 11th century and completed two centuries later. It is entirely faced with grey and white marble and is partly Romanesque and partly Gothic. The 13th-century **Campanile** is a fine example of Ligurian architecture. The tripartite interior of the church is decorated with 12th- and 13th-century *frescoes* and important sculptures.

Above: the Malaspina Castle overlooks the city of Massa.

The shipping port of Carrara used to export marble throughout the world.

ACADEMY OF FINE ARTS

An institution concerned with the teaching of art, the Academy of Fine Arts in Carrara came into being in 1769 to encourage the development of the marble industry and related arts in the Apuan Alps. Housed in its gallery of plaster casts are copies of famous originals, such as those seen here, and the works of famous artists such as, for example, Canova's plaster casts. Other items exhibited include artefacts from the archaeological site in Luni and the Roman Fantiscritti tabernacle.

The area of Tuscany around Carrara is of international importance for the marble that is quarried in the Apuan Alps mountains. For centuries artists, both famous and lesser known, have come from all over the world to make use of this rare marble – from Michelangelo to Canova and Carlo Fontana as well as many contemporary artists. Used in construction for both architectural and decorative purposes, as well as in the chemical and glass industries, Tuscan marble is found extensively in the Roman Pantheon, in Versailles and in some of the most modern buildings of the Arab States, Australia, and the United States. Many very attractive varieties are extracted in large quantities from the quarries including white "statuario", "arabescato", "pavonazzo" and Carrara "cipollino".

The scenery experienced on a tour around the quarries in the provinces of Lucca and Massa Carrara has a truly dramatic impact. In particular, however, it is a reminder of the immense human effort that for centuries the marble industry has required of the labourers, quarrymen and polishers who work in close contact with this hazardous environment every day. Some quarries such as Fantiscritti and Colonnata date from Roman times. The extraction and processing of this precious stone is documented in the **Fantiscritti Quarry-Museum.**

THE MARBLE
of the Apuan Alps

CONTENTS